The Abingdon Women's Preaching Annual

Series 2
Year B

Compiled and Edited by

Leonora Tubbs Tisdale

Abingdon Press
Nashville

THE ABINGDON WOMEN'S PREACHING ANNUAL

Copyright © 1999 by Abingdon Press

This book is printed on recycled, acid-free paper.

ISBN 0-687-08183-1

99 00 01 02 03 04 05 06 07 08 — 10 9 8 7 6 5 4 3 2 1

MANUFACTURED IN THE UNITED STATES OF AMERICA

In Loving Memory of

Lucy Atkinson Rose

1947–1997

Passionate preacher and teacher of preachers

Admired colleague, scholar, and challenger of the status quo

Advocate for women

Lover of family, friends, and world

Disciple of Jesus Christ

(Lucy Rose was also coeditor of the first series of *The Abingdon
Women's Preaching Annual*.)

Contents

Introduction

Women's Ways of Preaching" is the title of a course I regularly teach for pastors and seminarians. I first designed the course about ten years ago because of a need I perceived among clergy-women for "safe space" in which they could develop and expand their own gifts as preachers while also discussing issues of concern related to women and preaching. In this course many women (and a few brave men) have wrestled with issues ranging from authority in the pulpit (Do women exercise authority differently than men, and if so, how, why, and to what effect?), to gender and verbal communication issues (Do the patterns sociolinguists observe in women's and men's everyday speech carry over into the pulpit, and if so, to what effect?), to the role of personal experience in preaching (Do women, as many studies suggest, use more personal examples and illustrations in the pulpit than men? And if so, what are the positive contributions and the liabilities associated with such usage?).

Although I began teaching "Women's Ways of Preaching" because of a perceived need, I have continued teaching it for an additional reason: I love teaching it. I love hearing women tell the stories of their own calls, painful though those stories may be. I love hearing women discuss preaching issues of special concern to them—with candor, vivacity, and good humor. And I love hearing women preach. I especially delight in the rich diversity of perspectives and insights, stories and images, forms and styles, commitments and challenges women can now bring to a place that so long denied them, and their gifts, a hearing.

So when Abingdon Press asked me to edit the second series in *The Abingdon Women's Preaching Annual*, I jumped at the chance to do so. In some ways, putting together this volume has been like putting together a "Women's Ways of Preaching" class. Included in the class are people from a diversity of denominational, geographical, and racial-ethnic backgrounds, each of whom is seeking faithfully to interpret the gospel in her own unique ministry context. While an overt discussion of issues among the participants is lacking, many of those same issues are still implicitly present—informing the ways in which these women interpret biblical texts, form their sermons, and assert their own voices as preachers. What is most like a "Women's Ways of Preaching" class, however, is that you, the readers, get to sit back and listen for yourselves to the marvelously diverse ways in which eighteen women proclaim the gospel. And, since they are wrestling with the very same lectionary texts many of you will wrestle with over the course of the coming year, I hope their sermons will have the added benefit of priming the pumps of your own homiletical imaginations.

I haven't yet told you the biggest reason I love teaching "Women's Ways of Preaching." The reason is this: On their better preaching days, the women in these classes have, through their imaginative and faithful proclamation, made me want to be not only a better preacher, but also a better disciple of the Christ whose gospel we proclaim. As a new "class" finds voice through the pages of this volume, may it be so for you, too, dear readers. May it be so for you, too.

Leonora Tubbs Tisdale
Fall (Ordinary Time) 1998
Princeton Theological Seminary
Princeton, New Jersey

First Sunday of Advent

Joan Delaplane, O.P.

Isaiah 64:1-9: In a time of despair the people, aware of their sinfulness, plead with God for mercy.

Psalm 80:1-7, 17-19: A psalm of communal lament, acknowledging sin, promising repentance, and seeking God's salvation and restoration.

1 Corinthians 1:3-9: God is faithful, and it was God who called you to fellowship with Jesus Christ, our Lord.

Mark 13:24-37: Apocalyptic writing with foreboding imagery, but also with God's promise of victory in the end. In the meantime, there is the admonition to watch, be ready.

REFLECTIONS

Advent, a time of waiting, takes on a special poignancy this year in anticipation of the new millennium. Regardless of religious convictions, the world is focused on *time*. Some individuals are fearful of the end time. The readings from Isaiah and Psalm 80 strike me as being particularly relevant to this fear. When has a world so desperately needed to acknowledge sin and our need for God?

Christians are reminded that we are living in between times: that is, between "Christ has come" and "Christ will come again." For us the gift of time calls for a hope-filled response that brings light to the world's darkness, hope to despair, energy to ennui.

Instead of the usual Advent emphasis upon a people's waiting, perhaps the focus this Advent ought to be upon God's waiting. God is waiting for us to grasp more fully the reality that God has entered our history and truly is Emmanuel, God with us. This God will not go away until all creatures and creation are caught up in God's redeeming love.

11

A SERMON BRIEF

It must have been at least a thousand years since there has been so much talk about *time*, especially with a focus on a feared end time. As the new millennium approaches, the church itself enters into its annual Advent period of waiting and anticipation with a special poignancy.

Americans, especially, are not very good at this waiting aspect of life. We are accustomed to living in an age of immediacy. Microwaves, Xerox machines, and computers have trained us to believe that our wants and needs can be satisfied in minutes, sometimes seconds. Three months of winter can seem endless; nine months of a difficult pregnancy may seem an eternity. Desire for immediate gratification leads some down the path of drugs, sexual promiscuity, divorce, restlessness, and boredom.

How we wait and for what we wait make a difference in our experience of time. For those who wait with fear or anxiety, the test results from the doctor, a pink slip from work, or the death of a loved one, time can feel like an eternal dread. On the contrary, the excitement and anticipation of expecting a letter or a visit from a loved one, a long-desired baby, or a hard-earned graduation or promotion can make the wait as life-giving as the completed reality. Often the difference lies in a sense of hope.

Advent is, of all things, a time of hope! Early Christians were known by how they loved one another; today's Christians need to give witness to how we hope. In spite of all that calls us to despair, Christians hope because we believe in Emmanuel. We have not been left alone. Every moment of time is a gift to us to recognize and celebrate God's saving love and power at work, bringing about the fullness of God's reign. Every moment of time is an opportunity to give God glory by a loving and caring response for all creation and for each of God's creatures.

Yet hope can be a hard commodity to come by during this season where the darkness of the days often accentuates the gloom many find within. Abundant tree lights and glittering ornaments do little to relieve the depression some people feel at this time of year. And ironically, the artificial gaiety surrounding us at Christmas seems to accentuate the loneliness and emptiness in a singular way.

The people of Isaiah's time knew what it was to be living in a time of despair. In their case, despair had been brought about by their own sinfulness and forsaking of God's ways. They knew that their only

12

path to hope lay in God's deliverance from their sinfulness and from their desperate need. Claiming their relationship with God as Abba, Father/Mother, they cried out: "O that you would tear open the heavens and come down" (Isa. 64:1). They begged God the potter, who had first fashioned them, to forgive their iniquity, and to fashion them anew.

One look at our daily newspaper or five minutes of listening to the TV news readily enables us to recognize the relevancy of the Isaiah passage for contemporary times. Can we acknowledge our sinfulness: our greed, racism, sexism, violence, power struggles, abuse of children and elderly, lack of respect for human life and for creation, alienation from one another? Can we recognize our desperation enough to let ourselves be pliable in the hands of our loving potter who can mold us, shape us anew?

But such surrender must not be interpreted as a call for a passive stance. Six times in the last four verses of today's Gospel reading, we are admonished to stay awake, be alert, watch. This very active response suggests that instead of our waiting this Advent, God is waiting for us to wake up to the truth that God has entered our history. Emmanuel, God with us, is waiting for us to recognize where God is saying yes and where God is saying no in this time and to respond. We are called to a state of readiness.

My sister suffered from a brain tumor for eighteen years. She had a card at her bedroom door that read, "Call me when you're ready, God, but, please God, make me ready when you call!" And ready she was as a woman who persevered in faith, in hope, in love for God, God's people, and God's creation.

Unfortunately, it is often the dying person who begins to treasure every moment of life. A few years ago I was driving with a friend who was preparing to go to Germany to see her thirty-three-year-old sister-in-law who was dying of cancer. "I don't know what to say to her, nor to my brother who is so crazy about her," Agnes said. "I don't know what you should say, Agnes," I had to reply. "I only know that they are probably both treasuring the gift of the day. Here we are driving along; we could be killed in a car crash today. The question is, are we treasuring the gift of this day and living it fully?" The phone call came two weeks later. Agnes had been killed in a car crash in Germany on her way to visit her sister-in-law. I thought of our last conversation.

"Our lives are as brief as the hyphen between the dates on a gravestone," said David Buttrick (David G. Buttrick, *Preaching Jesus Christ:*

13

An Exercise in Homiletic Theology [Philadelphia: Fortress, 1988], 75). From God's perspective, perhaps the same is true of the time between "Christ has come" and "Christ will come again." The major question remains: Are we living the hyphen fully? Are we awake, watchful, on guard for the many ways in which our God is daily adventing into our lives, supporting us, challenging us to bring the light of God's truth and love into this world's darkness?

"O house of Jacob, come, let us walk in the light of the LORD!" the psalmist cries (Isa. 2:5). As Christians we add, "let us radiate the light that is Christ for the world."

Many people have lost hope. They are disillusioned, and, yes, some are despairing that things can ever be different. Cuts in government aid, cuts in medical assistance, job losses, the poor getting poorer as some CEOs' salaries reach the obscene—all cause a sense of power-lessness, a feeling of impasse. It is such experiences, however, that can move us to recognize the need for God. Only God can change the scene, and God's will is to do it in and through those who have hope.

The sense of darkness and despair leads to ennui, to inaction, to paralysis. The reality of Advent, however, is the admonition to be on guard, be awake, be alert. God has chosen to need us to make God's love, God's presence, compassion, and power tangible. We cannot afford to be sleepwalkers. Time is too precious; God's people are too precious! Our lives are meant to make a difference in God's world, no matter how small that difference may seem to each of us. Maranatha!

SUGGESTIONS FOR WORSHIP

Call to Worship (adapted from Isaiah 9:2)

LEADER: The people who walked in darkness have seen a great light;

PEOPLE: Those who lived in a land of deep darkness—on them light has shined.

LEADER: Come, let us worship the God
Whose light brings hope to a weary world.

Prayer of Confession

Rouse your strength, O Shepherd of Israel, come and save us. We have been rebels who have resisted being clay in your loving hands. We have turned from you and sought to fashion our own lives. We have sinned. By your grace, we desire to never turn from you again. With life renewed, we shall invoke your name.

Assurance of Pardon
(adapted from Isaiah 40:1-2)

LEADER: Comfort, O comfort my people, says your God.
                  Speak tenderly to Jerusalem, and cry to her
                  that she has served her term, that her penalty is paid.
PEOPLE: **Thanks be to God.**

Benediction

"May the God of hope fill you with all joy and peace in believing, so that you may abound in hope by the power of the Holy Spirit" (Rom. 15:13). Go now to be Christ's light in this world's darkness; hope for this world's despair; energy for this world's ennui.

Second Sunday of Advent

Rhonda VanDyke Colby

Isaiah 40:1-11: Isaiah foretells one crying, "In the wilderness prepare the way of the LORD."

Psalm 85:1-2, 8-13: The psalmist declares that salvation is near. Love and faithfulness meet; righteousness and peace kiss.

2 Peter 3:8-15a: God's time is not necessarily our time. The day of the Lord will come like a thief. We look forward to a new heaven and new earth.

Mark 1:1-8: Isaiah has prophesied John's coming. John promises a greater one will come after him. John points past himself to Jesus with anticipation.

REFLECTIONS

Every Advent John the Baptist screams onto the scene of the lectionary. One year I had just had enough of the warbling wilderness wild man. I thought that I had said everything I ever wanted to say about John the Baptist. His "in your face" startling message had become for me just one more well-known anticipated reading. My mind began to wander as I imagined how God might clear a path through the expected and ordinary approach to old John and let him and his message sneak up on me again. How might our congregation be surprised into "watchfulness"? How might we be slowed down and brought up short by an "in your face" messenger of a different kind? How might a startling stranger make the rough places plain and smooth out the wrinkles in our preconceptions about Advent/Coming? What would it take to point us beyond the messenger all the way to Jesus?

A few worshipers, slow to pick up on the imaginative nature of the sermon, were quick to admonish me about the dangers of talking to strangers and holding other people's babies. Still others asked, "Is that a true story?" I let them know that while the story had no basis in fact it was completely true. The Incarnate One is still becoming flesh. Watch! Be aware! Don't miss the things that point the way through our wilderness.

A SERMON BRIEF

Encounter at the K Mart

I always wanted to meet John the Baptist, this desert wild man who lived on locusts and honey, who announced that Jesus was coming and that people had better get ready. Well, I got the chance. I met John the Baptist the other day. I met him at the K Mart.

When I drove by the corner of Glenside and Broad Streets I looked for the man I've gotten used to seeing there. He holds a sign that reads, "I'll work for food." But this time he wasn't there. Someone else was in his place. This new guy looked just as disheveled but quite a bit wilder in the eyes. He held a sign made out of a torn-up cardboard box. It read, "It's time for a change."

I passed within two feet of him as I turned into the parking lot. He caught my eye for a moment and held my gaze as I made the turn, almost causing a minivan pile up. But to be honest, once I was in the store I didn't think of him again.

I got my cart and combed the store for all the essentials. More clear bulbs for the window candles, a few more extension cords, Christmas-patterned paper towels. Then into the checkout line where I exchanged holiday pleasantries with other hurried shoppers while I scratched a couple of items off my "to do" list.

Before picking up my bags I reached into my wallet for some extra change. I have a personal holiday policy of never passing a Salvation Army kettle without putting something in it. I wondered if my policy was really one of generosity or if it simply helped me avoid the guilt I felt when I passed by a kettle and the collector wished me "Merry Christmas" anyway.

With packages up to my chin, a fist full of pennies, and a swoosh of the automatic doors, I was out of the building. I immediately heard the bell; but there was no kettle, only John the Baptist ringing the bell and still holding his sign, "It's time for a change." He didn't look like an official of the Salvation Army, but who am I to judge?

"Nice sign," I said. "If it's change you want I've got some right here in my hand." I thought it was witty. He was clearly not amused.

"Are you prepared?" he asked me with intimidating intensity.

"Well, not yet. That's what all these packages are about. I've got a lot of decorating to do. And my husband and I have our annual Christmas open house, and I haven't even started baking. It's more than a little overwhelming. So, I've started a list of things I simply must do to be prepared."

"Let me help you," he said. Again he held my gaze. I wondered what he could do to lighten my burden. "Let me help you take your packages to your car. Then I'll buy you a cup of coffee."

"Wait a minute. You're the one standing out in the cold with a sign. I thought I was supposed to buy you the coffee."

He didn't say a word. He just tucked his sign under his arm and unburdened me of some of my baggage. When I opened the car door he saw one of my most-prized possessions there on the seat. He said, "Better bring that with you." So I picked up my daily planner and followed him back into the K Mart.

There in the snack bar over a hot cup of coffee he leafed his way through my life—my lists and schedule. Most of the time he just shook his head. Occasionally he would let out a disapproving grunt. Once he mumbled something sarcastic under his breath. I felt like a school girl watching a teacher grade a test and realizing that I hadn't answered a single question correctly.

Then he brightened up. "O.K. Here's something I like," he finally said. "'Get rid of clutter. Clear a path.' Tell me about that."

I explained that my den was strewn with boxes of Christmas decorations that had been hiding in my garage since we had moved in that summer. I needed time to sort out the Santa place mats from the nativity scenes and to clear a path through my den.

His shoulders fell with disappointment, and he went back to his review. When he had finished reading, he turned to a new page in my planner. Then he reached in his pocket and pulled out an old pencil stub. It was the kind you use to keep score in miniature golf, and it was worn down to half its size but freshly sharpened as if prepared for this moment. He smoothed the paper, being sure to flatten any bends, wrinkles, or raised places. He then touched the tip of his pencil to his tongue and wrote for me a new list. I watched in silence as this vagabond in the suburban wilderness wrote intently on the pages of my priorities.

At the top of the page he wrote, "DO LIST." Number 1 said, "Hold a baby." What a strange instruction. Before I could ask him to explain I heard a woman next to me let out a squeal. Her toddler had climbed up a display to get a closer look at a stuffed Tickle-Me-Something-or-Other. The display began to teeter. Without a word between us she passed me her newborn to hold as she ran after her little climber.

I looked down at the bundle she had placed in my arms. He was so tiny, so fragile. He reached for my face with his delicate hand. The Muzak on the store's sound system played an instrumental version of "What Child Is This," and for a moment I wasn't in K Mart but in Bethlehem. I was holding close to me the tiny body of the one whose body would be broken for me. The tiny hand reaching for me was the hand that would reach out to embrace the cosmos and then bear a nail on my behalf.

Too soon an announcement of a "blue-light special" broke into the moment and the mother returned for her baby. I glanced back at my planner and saw Number 2: "Wonder." Wonder? Wonder what? Wonder why God chose a helpless little baby to bring salvation into a hostile world? Wonder why after thousands of years we still haven't gotten the message? Wonder when Christ will come again? I wondered. I wondered what to wonder. And I wondered some more.

The announcement came over the loudspeaker. K Mart was closing. Bring final purchases to the register. Where had the time gone? How long had I been sitting there? I looked around but didn't see John anywhere. I glanced down at the third item on my DO LIST. "Look to the stars." What did that mean?

As I walked outside I heard a plane overhead. I looked up to see a clear sky full of stars. There were thousands of them. More beautiful than the lights on any Christmas tree. They took my breath. And I hadn't had to work to put them up there. I hadn't had to untangle the cords or check for dud star-bulbs. This light display required no extension cord. It was placed there for me as a gift, an unmerited spectacle of wonder.

There in the K Mart parking lot, looking into the night sky, I had a strong sense that I had been looking in the wrong place for Christmas. I had been too busy rushing around to look up. I had been so busy worrying about what I had to do that I forgot to appreciate what had already been done for me. I had been so preoccupied with following the crowd that I had neglected to follow the star.

As I gazed into the sky it seemed that one star was shining a little brighter than all the rest. Remembering the stranger's admonition I followed it. Perhaps it would lead me to Bethlehem. As I walked

19

through the cold night, to my amazement, the light of the star seemed to fall upon . . . my minivan. In the starlight I could just see the cardboard sign, tucked under my windshield wiper. "It's time for a change," the sign reminded me.

No matter how your Advent season is going so far, it is not too late. It is not too late to hold a child, to wonder, to look up, to follow a star. It's not too late for a change. Take it from me. I know it for a fact. I learned it the night I met John the Baptist at the K Mart.

SUGGESTIONS FOR WORSHIP

Call to Worship

ONE: In this season of mystery,
MANY: **Let us watch for God's surprises!**
ONE: Steadfast love and faithfulness will meet;
              righteousness and peace will kiss each other.
MANY: **The ordinary will encounter the extraordinary.**
ONE: And something . . .
MANY: **Something extraordinary will happen.**
ONE: Watch!

Prayer of Confession

O Surprising One, we confess that we continually look for you in the ordinary places: on the front of Christmas cards, in the plastic nativity scenes on our neighbors' lawns, in familiar carols, in the church we call home. We watch for the blanketed babe with the omniscient smile and the heavenly glow. So sure are we of how you will appear to us that we miss your incarnation where we do not expect it. We have failed to see you enfleshed in our enemies. We have not recognized you in faces that do not look like our own in their color and shape and age. We confess that we have refused to acknowledge your incarnation in ourselves for fear that to have Christ in us would be too costly.

Forgive our narrowness. Help us to watch. Teach us to recognize. Surprise us even today, even this hour, by breaking into the ordinariness of our worship so that we might see you anew. O come, O come, Emmanuel.

Assurance of Pardon

Hear the good news! Christ is coming! With or without our recognition, God is becoming flesh. Even when we see no need for God, God sees our need and comes—again and again. Thanks be to God!

Benediction

Stay awake!
  Look out!
    Look up!
      Look in!
        And wonder.
        Christ is coming!

Third Sunday of Advent

Yvette Flunder and Valerie Brown-Troutt

Isaiah 61:1-4, 8-11: "The spirit of the Lord GOD is upon me . . . the LORD . . . has sent me . . . to proclaim liberty to the captives."

Luke 1:47-55: The Magnificat of Mary.

1 Thessalonians 5:16-24: "Rejoice always . . . give thanks in all circumstances . . . hold fast to what is good."

John 1:6-8, 19-28: John testifies concerning the Messiah, declaring that he (John) is "the voice of one crying out in the wilderness."

REFLECTIONS

The theology of those at the center of society often seeks to characterize people on the edge as enemies of God. This is especially true when individuals or groups unrepentantly refuse to conform to the dominant definition of normativeness. Overcoming oppressive theology, or a theology that excludes certain people, is critical in creating a Christian community for people on the periphery.

Marginalized people respond to a community of openness and inclusiveness where other people from the edge gather. Such an atmosphere welcomes people and makes them feel safer to be who they are. A liberating theology of acceptance must be embodied by a liberating Christian community.

Contempt for the church and for all things religious often stems from exposure to oppressive theology, biblical literalism and unyielding tradition. A person, church, or society can do extreme harm in the name of God and virtue and with the "support" of scripture. Oppressive theology is a ball and chain on the heart of the body of Christ. With it we can keep each other in bondage.

Isaiah 61 speaks of one who will come to bring good news to the oppressed and to proclaim liberty to the captives. Jesus echoed Isaiah's eternal freedom song as his foundation for ministry. This foundation must also be the foundation of an oppression-free Christian community. How can we be the church of Jesus unless we reflect the ministry of Jesus?

It is crucial in the formation of community that those who were and are oppressed seek to overcome the theological millstones tied around their necks. It is equally important for others not to adopt pejorative assumptions toward those in the community who are different, and thus pass on the sickness of oppressive theology. Our principal message should be, The year of Jubilee has come!

A SERMON BRIEF

Overcoming Oppressive Theology

Theos/logos, "God words" or words about God, are not etched in granite; they metamorphose with time. All of us see things a bit differently than we saw them ten years ago, and certainly our theology has progressed since we first met Jesus.

Some of us are *Meeting Jesus Again for the First Time*—the title of a book I read last year (Marcus J. Borg, *Meeting Jesus Again for the First Time: The Historical Jesus and the Heart of Contemporary Faith* [San Francisco: HarperCollins, 1994]). We met Jesus at an earlier time, before we experienced much of life, and we thought we knew all about him—only to find out that this walk with Jesus must be experiential. You must walk with Jesus to know Jesus. And as we walk his way of suffering, our theology changes.

The church of Jesus Christ is also in the midst of change, some of it for the better, and some of it for the worse. Some of our theology binds, while some sets free.

Today our Old Testament reading from Isaiah 61 reminds us of the purposes for which Jesus came. Jesus, in inaugurating his own ministry here on earth, read from this very same portion of Isaiah's scroll in the synagogue one Sabbath morning. He said the spirit of the sovereign God was upon him for these purposes:

—to preach good tidings to the meek;
—to bind up the broken hearted;

— to proclaim liberty to the captives;

— to open the prisons of them that are bound;

— to proclaim the acceptable year—the year of Jubilee.

During this season of Advent, we must remind ourselves of the purposes for which Christ came, for these must also be our purposes. All ministry that purports to proclaim the good news of Jesus Christ must pass this litmus test: Does the ministry promote us, our views, our philosophy and dogma, or does it represent the real Jesus?

Certainly there is oppressive theology being preached in the body of Christ. Listen carefully to the television, the radio; read carefully the books and the mail. You will see three distinct basic teachings that are at the root of oppressive theology.

1. Nationality of God

In this country we often hear that "God is the God of our nation. We are the people God loves most. Let's get America back to God." It is as though we have exclusive rights to God. Indeed, in our nation, what is called Christianity is often Americanism. "God must prefer my country because I do." With this type of thinking the majority race can close the borders, oppress minorities, or justify foreign wars because "God is our God and prefers us."

The political parties think God belongs to them. White folk think God belongs to them. Israelis think they own God; Arabs try to own God. And we African Americans sometimes feel God loves us much more than anyone else (at least more than anyone who is different than we are).

Denominations, too, take on this mentality. Within the Christian church alone we teach baptism in Jesus' name, in the name of the Trinity, for adults only, for children only, by immersion, by sprinkling, as necessary for salvation, and as a prerequisite for the gift of the Holy Ghost. Each denomination feels that it has *the* revelation of God, and therefore, "If I am right, you must be wrong." Turf wars abound for ownership of the real word of God. And it is amazing the divisions these wars cause.

Yet our God is not a God of any one nation, nor of any one denomination. Nations are formed to facilitate the needs of their citizens. Denominations are set up to facilitate the work of the church on earth. Human beings, not buildings or organizations, are called to be a habitation for the Spirit of God. And therefore, we must preach a gospel that heals and brings wholeness to the person.

Is the gospel intended to imprison people to a nation or to a denomination? Isaiah preached liberty to the captives and freedom to those in bondage. This is the gospel.

2. Preconceived Interpretation

Another theology that oppresses is the theology that is born out of our own preconceived interpretations of the Bible. Often we go to the Bible already sure we know what it says. We have decided God is for this and against that, and we approach the scriptures looking for those passages that defend our own positions. It doesn't matter whether we take passages out of context or not. All that is important is defending our own point of view.

What would happen if we took a different approach to biblical study? If we came to the study of scripture seeking to understand the times, the context, the politics, the culture, the religion, and the social norms represented by thousands of years of history in the word? Then we would be better equipped to make the scriptures relevant to the times in which we live rather than having them simply feed our own biases and prejudices. Rightly divining the truth would help us know what was intended for literal translation, and what was given to teach a spiritual principle.

The good news spoken by the prophet Isaiah supports a guiding principle for our interpretation. Good interpretation, good theology, brings joy, gives comfort, and produces righteousness.

3. Inherited Oppression

And last, to my sisters and brothers of the African diaspora: We have been a historically oppressed people. We were taught the word of God by good religious folk who could sing "Amazing Grace" on the deck of a slave ship—the same people who felt fully justified by that word to sell us, brand us, beat us, and sell off our children. Our understanding of a God that could allow such atrocities would have to leave us feeling inferior.

And how does an inferior group of people feel superior? The oppressed become oppressors. It is a learned behavior. Light-colored folk feel superior to dark folk. Skinny folk feel superior to fat folk. Educated folk feel superior to undereducated folk. Men lord over women, "haves" lord over the "have nots." The pulpit becomes a place of monarchy, not ministry. And African Americans who got their opportunity through affirmative action are now speaking against it.

The truth of the matter is this: We will not be truly free until we adopt a theology that does not oppress anyone. Oppressive theology is a chain upon our hearts, and with it we have also kept one another in chains.

So let us heed the words of the prophet Isaiah and of Jesus. Let's have a year of Jubilee! Let's lift the clouds of judgment and allow a celebration of diversity to shine forth. Let's tear down the walls of partition and loose the Spirit of God to flow from church to temple to cathedral to mission to prayer group. Let's open the prisons of those that are bound. Let's set each other free.

SUGGESTIONS FOR WORSHIP

Prayer/Song

Stony the road we trod,
Bitter the chast'ning rod
Felt in the days when hope unborn had died;
Yet with a steady beat
Have not our weary feet
Come to the place for which our fathers sighed?

We have come over a way that with tears has been watered,
We have come, treading our path through the blood of the slaughtered,
Out from the gloomy past, till now we stand at last
Where the white gleam of our bright star is cast.
(James Weldon Johnson, "Lift Every Voice and Sing," *The New Progressive Baptist Hymnal* [Washington, D.C.: Progressive National Baptist Convention, 1977])

Prayer

Lord of liberty and love,
We know you hate oppression of all kinds.
We seek to reflect you in the earth.
Cleanse us from our unrighteousness.
Direct our work in truth according to your word.

Lord, we seek to live our lives in covenant with you.

We seek to be seeds of blessing for your glory everywhere we are.
In our homes, make us a blessing.
In our neighborhoods, make us a blessing.
In our communities, make us a blessing.
Among the nations of the world, make us a blessing.

We pray that all those who see us will acknowledge
that we are the seeds that the Lord has used to bring blessing. Amen.

Benediction

As you leave, my sisters and brothers, go greatly rejoicing in the Lord.

As you leave, my sisters and brothers, go clothed in the garments of salvation.

As you leave, my sisters and brothers, go robed in God's robe of righteousness.

As you leave, my sisters and brothers, go adorned with love for all people.

As you leave, my sisters and brothers, go living your lives so that righteousness and praise spring forth among all the nations. Amen.

Fourth Sunday of Advent

Anna Carter Florence

---

2 Samuel 7:1-11, 16: God's covenant with David: God will make of his line an everlasting house.

Luke 1:46b-55: Mary's Magnificat, or Psalm 89:1-4, 19-26: The psalm on which Mary's Magnificat is based.

Luke 1:26-38: The story of the annunciation.

Romans 16:25-27: Paul's "final doxology"; the secret of the ages is revealed in Jesus Christ.

REFLECTIONS

After years and years of waiting, the annunciation turns the tide. Here, at last, is the day you have been longing for, O Israel! Here is the time you knew must be, the time for which you prayed and yearned and raged and wept! Here is the secret of the ages, here is the great mystery of all time, and here are the angels with all the appropriate heraldry to announce it! Now, if you will only sit tight for another thirty years and nine months, we'll be ready to roll.

The annunciation demands patience, the patience of a mother. The messiah does not simply appear, fully formed. He has to be carried and labored over, born and raised, loved and nurtured, taught and disciplined. He comes to be through the love and care of a human family, and that requires what it has always required: more love and time than you thought you had to give. But that is the announcement. God in Christ is coming to live among us as one of us. God in Christ requires no army's protection; only a mother's and a father's love.

Announcements don't usually seem to call for a response. They are statements of immediate fact that concern the entire group. "Listen

28

up, everybody; I have something to tell you," one might begin. Yet it is a curious thing that Mary responds at the end of Gabriel's message. She agrees to be part of things. She buys into the vision. I have always wondered if there were other young women whom Gabriel approached first, who perhaps said, "No, thank you." Does God's incarnation require our assent?

In this sermon, I thought about what it means to announce the good news, and about Mary and the conflicting messages we often hear about her. There are so many, and there are so many renderings of Mary in both art and kitsch, that this is one of those passages to which we automatically bring a lot of baggage. I made an attempt to distinguish those images in my mind. What is the nature of the power of God's announcement to a young woman like Mary?

A SERMON BRIEF

Let me be honest. As a Protestant woman, I am completely fascinated with Mary. Or maybe it would be more accurate to say that I am completely fascinated by the attention she gets from our Roman Catholic and Eastern Orthodox friends. That there is a complete liturgical tradition and culture devoted to Mary, a tradition in which I have no part and of which I am largely ignorant, sometimes makes me feel like the child of immigrants: I know my parents used to speak that language and follow those customs, but they don't make sense for me, here, in the new world. And that was surely the goal of the Reformers, wasn't it?—to so thoroughly eliminate every trace of Mary from word and sacrament that before long, people would not remember the old practices and would not be able to hand them down to their children. It only takes a generation or two of neglect, after all, to lose a culture. Sometimes that's how I feel: as if I've lost a culture that might have nourished me in ways I can't even imagine.

To be fair, I am Protestant enough that I can sympathize with some of the Reformers' original complaints about Mary and the intercession of saints. At the time of the Reformation, people often prayed to God not directly but through a saint who might petition on their behalf, and the Queen of Heaven was a clear favorite. The Reformers, mincing no words, thought this sheer stupidity; Calvin called it a "horrid sacrilege" to call upon any intermediary but Christ (John Calvin, *Institutes of the Christian Religion*, III.xx.22 [Philadelphia: Westminster,

1960]). So the sanctuaries were stripped of all decoration, the liturgy rewritten, and the prayers simplified into forms we would immediately recognize today. In the process, Mary lost her throne. All that remains of her in our tradition is what we read in scripture.

And what is that, exactly? Who is this young woman from Nazareth who one day, out of the blue, finds herself addressed by God? Whose very proper engagement is suddenly shrouded in scandal? Whose quiet certainty convinces her fiancé not to dismiss her, but to stand by her and raise the child he did not conceive? Whose acceptance of God's plan for her life fills her with a vision for all creation that pours out of her in song? Who is she?

In many ways, that's an impossible question. Mary is what we make of her, and that includes both good and bad. She can be the shining example of human obedience or the stunning example of blind obedience. She can be a model of courage to inspire all people or a model of passivity to keep women down. She can be the best metaphor we have for the way God enters our messy human lives or she can be the woman on the pedestal whose purity has to be protected at all costs, even the cost of her humanness. Mary is and has been all these things. She is nothing short of an icon.

An icon. That's a word that conjures up images of the second commandment and idol worship. Protestants tend to be wary of icons. We don't use them and therefore don't understand them. They are part of our immigrant past. But what have we lost in giving up that past? How can Mary be an icon who transcends all our stereotypes?

In the harbor of Gloucester, Massachusetts, there is a Roman Catholic Church called Our Lady of the Seas. The steeple bears a statue of Mary, looking out to sea, with a fishing boat cradled in her hands. It is an image of tremendous power for this community because Gloucester is a fishing village, and in its three-hundred-year history, more than thirty thousand fisherman—many of them Portuguese and Italian immigrants—have lost their lives at sea. Even today, fishing remains one of the most dangerous occupations, and one of the poorest. When the storms come and the radios give out, there is nothing to do but pray. For generations, fishing wives have gone to the church to pray for their husbands' safety, and fishermen have carried the statue down to the harbor for the annual blessing of the fleet. Mary, Our Lady of the Seas. She offers no miracles. She can only cradle the boat as it puts to sea, as she once cradled her baby who was destined to die. In her strength, her resolve, the community finds its own.

The Mary we read about in scripture is the same Mary who stands watch over the Gloucester Harbor. At least I hope she is, because if the story of the annunciation is to mean anything to us, it must *announce*, today, to the fisherman of Gloucester, that God in Christ has defeated the powers of this world. It must announce, today, to migrant workers in Texas, that God in Christ has brought down the mighty from their thrones. It must announce, today, to Asian women forced into prostitution, that God in Christ has lifted up the lowly. Our Lady of the Seas, Our Lady of the Fields, Our Lady of the Brothels—it is the same Mary, the same peasant girl who heard the angel, and accepted the news, and set her face toward a future in God's hands.

We do not need to keep her pure. The story tells us that she left pure behind. She left safe behind. She left proper and comfortable and secure far behind her, and traded them for a vision of God incarnate in every single human life, no matter how poor or dirty or lost at sea. The Mary we read about in scripture is not on some pedestal, but on a steeple, watching the fleet as it leaves the harbor. And the prayer on her lips is anything but meek; it is joyful anticipation, uttered through tears and gritted teeth, of the day when every soul shall magnify the Lord.

"Here am I, the servant of the Lord; let it be with me according to your word" (Luke 1:38).

SUGGESTIONS FOR WORSHIP

Call to Worship

LEADER: Hear, O Israel: the Lord your God is one God!
PEOPLE: **Hear, O Israel: God will make of you one everlasting house.**
LEADER: Hear, O Israel: the Mighty One has done great things for us!
PEOPLE: **Hear, O Israel: God has raised up the lowly, and filled the hungry with good things.**
ALL: **Let our souls magnify the Lord! Let us worship God!**

Prayer of Confession

Eternal God, you have given us so much, and we have failed to be faithful. You give us mystery, and we deny its power. You give us

31

prophecy, and we refuse its calling. You give us wisdom, and we behave foolishly. You shower us with blessings, and we sell them for the sake of our own vain desires. Forgive us, God. Help us do what is right, and say what is true, and love as passionately as you love. Give us the mind of Christ so that we might bring peace to this world. We pray in Jesus' name. Amen.

Assurance of Pardon

Sisters and brothers, the good news is this: that while we make of this earth a poor thing, God in Christ is coming into the world to make straight all our paths, and to prepare the Lord's way. Hear the gospel this day: In Jesus Christ, you are forgiven. Thanks be to God.

Benediction (adapted from Romans 16:25-27)

Now may the gospel of Jesus Christ strengthen you,
The revelation of the mystery of the ages sustain you,
And the prophecy of God's holy word keep you in faith and hope,
both now and forevermore. Amen.

Christmas Eve

Catherine Erskine Boileau

Isaiah 9:2-7: God promises light to shine in the darkness, through a child born unto us.

Psalm 96: All creation is renewed by singing a new song to the Lord.

Titus 2:11-14: The coming of Christ releases us from bondage to sin.

Luke 2:1-14 (15-20): Luke's compelling story of Christ's birth.

REFLECTIONS

Walter Wangerin, Jr., tells us that when it comes to sharing the Christmas story, we ought to do so only with the reverence of hushed tones and whispers and hearts that radiate love (Walter Wangerin, Jr., "The Christmas Story," in *The Manger Is Empty: Stories in Time* [New York: HarperCollins, 1989]). What a glorious story of angelic visitors and stars and a new mother's ponderings! What else could we feel but wonder as we approach the manger, realizing for the first or hundredth time that God chose to break into our history, not with angelic armies or fire and brimstone, but as a tiny, helpless infant murmuring in the night?

But this is not just a story, it is our story. It is not just about shepherds and angels and Magi, but about us. And so the story is a mixture of darkness and light, grace and sin, judgment and mercy, love and violence. And this story is not just about any baby, it is about our baby. Isaiah's voice echoes through the centuries, "A child has been born for us, a son given to us" (9:6*a*).

What does it mean to accept our part in that "us"? Can we hear the whispered invitation that the child in the manger become not just the world's savior but our savior? Are we ready to be led by stars and innkeepers and angels to the manger community where there is no more "we and they," only "us"? Have we become part of the gathering that worships the child alongside all those beloved characters of the ancient story, or are we still standing back, aloof, watching and waiting, not ready to admit that we needed him to come?

A SERMON BRIEF

Giving birth is a community event. Oh, don't get me wrong. I'm not one of those courageous souls who invites the extended family and NBC into the labor and delivery room. In fact, I threatened my husband with bodily harm if he so much as went for a camera during our children's births. There is a reason I believe that the sign to the shepherds was a baby already born and lying in a manger, and not a pregnant woman. Poor Mary didn't need all those shepherds and wise men hanging around for the birth.

But as a pastor in a small town, my pregnancies were community events. There was no hiding my morning sickness as I crawled into the pulpit on Sunday mornings armed with ginger ale and nausea wristbands. My baby showers were congregational events, well attended by men and women alike. Gruff, retired trustees who had never before attended a shower stood sheepishly against the walls, waiting with childlike expectation until I opened their gifts. Young fathers stood in silent camaraderie with my husband. And in my quiet moments of pondering, I was moved by their celebration, for at some level I sensed that unto *us* these children had been born.

But isn't the birth of any child a communal event? When we hear of a child born to a coworker or neighbor, don't we also rejoice? We put signs in the front yard so that total strangers will know, "It's a Girl!" We send cards and put announcements in the paper, because somehow we understand the miracle of a new birth is God's gift to us all.

Why should it surprise us, then, that the sign of God's redemptive act is often the birth of a child? For Abraham, the sign of God's coming was Isaac; for Hannah, the sign was Samuel. For Isaiah and the whole people of God who stood thirsting for God's redemption, the promise again is a child. And the name of this child is "Wonderful Counselor, Mighty God, Everlasting Father, Prince of Peace."

What hope Judah must have had for this child! A child who would one day lead the nation out of the darkness of its brokenness and sin into the dawn of a restored covenant with God. A child whose reign would embrace both justice and mercy and whose rule would strike that delicate balance between gentleness and strength. If the birth of an ordinary child draws the community together in shared joy and wonder, how much more would this special child break down the "we-they" divisions within Israel and restore Israel to an "us" again? What songs must have greeted this child's coming!

Is it any wonder, then, that Isaiah's song echoes through the songs of the angels on that miraculous night when Jesus is born? We've all read the scholars who wisely warn us against jumping too quickly from Isaiah to Jesus. Isaiah isn't even mentioned in Luke's telling of the story. But how can we help hearing the strains of Isaiah's song reverberating through the Christmas story? Wouldn't our hearts sing it even if the lectionary chose a different Old Testament text for Christmas Eve? More than any other birth, doesn't this birth give all creation reason to rejoice? More than any other child, isn't this child given to us all?

But what about that "us" in the story? Deep down, aren't we just a little tempted to believe that the miraculous story belongs more to Mary and the shepherds than it does to *us*? Have we heard the angels call *our* name, just as they called Mary's? Have we really heard that this child is good news for *us*, just as he was for the shepherds? Have we, like Joseph, been able to accept that the story is about *us* even if our names aren't in the headlines?

"Us" is a key word in the Christmas story. "Us" makes the manger a personal invitation. "Us" means that our lives and this child's life are eternally intertwined. As long as this child belongs just to Mary and Joseph, we don't have to wonder why God lies before us in a trough filled with scratchy old hay, like a sack of feed for the animals.

The truth is we don't want to hear the "us" in Isaiah's song because we don't like having to admit that God had to go to such desperate measures to bring us back. We don't like to confess this Christmas that our lives are less than perfect, that deep down we're not quite as happy as we would like everyone to believe. There are wounds, cleverly hidden, festering in our hearts. There are secret pockets of bitterness, where the refreshing waters of forgiveness have simply dried up. There are the cobwebs of doubt, where we secretly wonder why the angels always sing for the house next door, but never for us. And if we admit to ourselves that we are the "us" to whom this child is given, we might also have to admit that we are the "us" for whom this Christ Child died. The reality of Isaiah's "us" is that this child in the manger didn't just come to us. He came for us.

In the movie *Field of Dreams*, a child of the sixties turned Iowa farmer suddenly hears a voice telling him to plow up his fields and build a baseball field. "If you build it, he will come," says the voice. Ray obeys the voice and finishes the field. The voice visits again, telling Ray, "Ease his pain." Mystified by whose pain he is supposed to heal, Ray begins a long search for the one who will be healed by this cornfield turned baseball diamond. One day, Ray's father, who had died before Ray had ever had a chance to build any kind of meaningful relationship with him, appears on the field for a game with the other ballplayers. With tears in his eyes, Ray believes he has finally found the one in need of healing. "Ease his pain," murmurs Ray. As his father steps across the field for which Ray labored, Ray says "It was you."

"No, Ray," says one of the players, gently. "It was you." It was for you.

It was for you that Jesus came. It was for your hurts, your sins, your failings, your broken heart, that he lay in the manger that night. It was for your doubt, your grief, your anger, that he gave it all, nothing held back. It was because you were in the dark and he wanted to be the light that would guide you back home. It was because you were deaf and he wanted you to hear. It wasn't just for the shepherds or for Mary or for the Magi that he came. It was for you. It was for you.

The transforming moment of Christmas comes when we claim our place at the manger. When we realize that the Christ Child has come, not just for the world, but for us. When we realize that Jesus came because of our sin, that he walked to the cross breathing our name. It is not just world peace he promises, but our peace. It is not just the world's story that needs to be changed, but our story. It is for our transgression the Christ Child will one day be pierced; it is for our iniquities he will be crushed.

But it is also the humble acceptance of this gift of manger and cross, grave and resurrection, that transforms the "we-they" attitude of our fractured world into a true "us." Around the manger, a new community is born. The excited shepherds share their story; a loving mother shares her son. The Magi give gifts; the innkeepers supply hay. Rich and poor, Gentile and Jew, migrant and landowner, male and female, are transformed into the kind of "us" possible only with the love of this child, the one called Prince of Peace. My prayer this

Christmas is that we will not only remember Isaiah's song, but also sing it with the joy of knowing that it is our song as well. My prayer is that we will be among those who are so transformed by that child sleeping in the manger that we shall be the seeds of that new community, a place where there is no more "we-they," only "us." My prayer is that throughout this coming year, we will be among those who see the fulfillment of Isaiah's song and Isaiah's hope and claim the promise of Isaiah's God.

"For a child has been born for *us*, a son given to *us*; authority rests upon his shoulders; and he is named Wonderful Counselor, Mighty God, Everlasting Father, Prince of Peace" (Isa. 9:6, emphasis added).

SUGGESTIONS FOR WORSHIP

Call to Worship

LEADER: There's a song in the air. Will you sing it?
PEOPLE: Let us sing to the Lord a new song.
LEADER: There's a star in the sky. Will you follow it?
PEOPLE: Let us abandon our darkness and embrace the light.
LEADER: There's a mother's deep prayer. Will you breathe it?
PEOPLE: Let us repent of our shallowness and ponder his coming.
LEADER: And a baby's low cry. Will you adore him?
PEOPLE: Let us worship the Lord Jesus Christ.
             (Adapted from Josiah G. Holland, "There's a Song in the Air," 1874)

Prayer of Confession

O God, our light, if ever there were a people who need your light, it is us. If ever there were a place where hope needed to be born, it is in the manger of our hearts. The work of your hands surrounds us, the miracle of your coming confronts us, but we remain weary of heart. We hear the songs of angels but cannot muster the joy to sing. You call us, like shepherds of old, to your manger to worship, but our minds wander.

O Jesus, who never tires of loving us, intervene in our history once more. Forgive our complacency. Come, be born in our hearts anew,

37

that your light might blaze through our lives, that nations might gather at your manger, and that your name might be exalted in all the earth. Amen.

Assurance of Pardon

The true home for Jesus on earth is not a manger but an open, repentant heart. Open your hearts, that you might find forgiveness for your sin and the salvation of your souls.

Benediction

LEADER: Go forth in joy! For unto us a child is born, unto us a son is given.

PEOPLE: **And his name shall be called Wonderful Counselor, Mighty God, Everlasting Father, Prince of Peace.**

First Sunday After Christmas

Gláucia Vasconcelos Wilkey

Isaiah 61:10–62:3: The prophet continues to sound forth the message of justice and care for the forgotten ones—a message that centuries later would be said to have been fulfilled in the coming of Jesus Christ (Luke 4). This passage is a song of hope of liberation from oppression, slavery, and warfare. Justice and hope are expressed in terms of visions of new garments, new status, a new name, new life, a new song. The rich imagery of this text informs and shapes our hearing of the other readings for the day.

Psalm 148: A joyful song of praise that is part of the set that concludes not only the fifth and last segment of the collection of books of psalms, but the psalter itself. Psalms 146 to 150 all begin and end with the same exclamations: "Hallelujah!" and "Praise the Lord!" Like the other four, this is a psalm in three parts including an invitation to praise, a reason for praise, and a concluding exclamation of praise. The uniqueness of this psalm is found in the powerful connection the psalmist makes between creation and salvation and the universality of God's grace ("Young men and women alike, old and young together! Let them praise the name of the Lord" [vv. 12-13*a*]). Sung in juxtaposition with the readings for the day, this psalm shines light on the whole of salvation history and on the incarnation of God in Jesus Christ.

Galatians 4:4-7: Continuing a discussion of the new ways of grace found in Christ, Paul uses evocative, poetic, and familiar images to distinguish this life from the old, law-shaped patterns of relationships. This text, often read on Christmas Day, engages the reader in the beauty and depth of the new relationship between God and humanity. It is, in fact, the gospel in a nutshell. God has sent God's son. The result is

. . .

reassuring: Those who belong to Christ are slaves no longer, but children of God, heirs with Christ of the fullness of God's riches. And the very spirit of the incarnate God confirms that adoption for those who once lived under the law.

Luke 2:22-40: The previous texts set the foundation for the culmination of readings for this day: the Luke story. It is a rich and illuminating story in which the listener is exposed to the basic and foundational themes of the gospel as seen through Luke's eyes. Jesus' parents are fulfilling the law of which Paul spoke to the Galatians, but there is much more to the scene: Grace and salvation are both foreseen and very present. The infant the parents bring to the Temple is seen by Simeon and Anna as the consolation of Israel and the "redemption of Jerusalem."

REFLECTIONS

The astonishing speech-acts of Simeon and Anna express anticipation of liberation, as they find in Jesus reinterpretation of the hopes of Israel. The presence of two representatives of the outcasts of Israel (old man, old woman and widow) as the ones to whom salvation is disclosed points to both the nature of the life of the child, and the nature of the fullness of the revelation of God in Jesus Christ. In the birth of a tiny baby, God's marvelous liberation has shown forth on earth—a liberation that issues both in songs of praise ("These eyes have seen salvation's dawn. . . .") and in lives transformed by the gift of freedom.

A SERMON BRIEF

Breaking Forth in Wonder

What a woman we meet in this Anna, introduced to us at the presentation of the baby Jesus in the Temple! She had much against her: she was a woman, a widow, and old. In society's eyes, she was of little importance. The cultural values of her time associated men with honor, and women with shame. In like manner, age was associated with weakness, female widowhood with need. While men were easily recognized as spiritual leaders, women's spirituality was more often than not viewed as contingent upon and even secondary to men's.

The Gospel story for this first Sunday after Christmas, however, continues the surprising revelation of the fullness God's grace manifested by Jesus' birth. In the birth of the Christ Child, a new era begins, and all creation is called to break forth in wonder. For the light of grace revealed in this child, Jesus, casts an aura upon all who encounter him. It is a light that radiates from the tiny person at the center of the scene described in the Gospel reading. It is a light that reflects upon old Simeon and causes all of us to see a new dimension, a new era. That new era also shines forth gloriously in old Anna's behavior.

In Anna's speech-act the old oppressive patterns of gender, age, and marital status begin to crumble. She has encountered the liberating God in Jesus. Through the lens of spiritual discernment she sees the promised salvation, a salvation that brings to flower the words of the ancient psalm for this day: "Young men and women alike, old and young together! Let them praise the name of the LORD" (Ps. 148:12-13*a*). And decades after the presentation of Jesus in the Temple, the apostle Paul can say confidently that Anna and all other people to whom society pays little or no honor—children, women, slaves, the elderly, the differently abled—all are in Jesus Christ equal before God. In fact, Paul claims that Anna is an heir with Christ of the fullness of God's riches. Such a gift of grace is enough to cause Anna—and all of us—to break forth in wonder before the incarnate God, Emmanuel.

In the moving tableau in the Temple, more attention is given to Simeon, who is said to have been guided by the Spirit. It is Simeon who takes the child in his arms and blesses Mary and Joseph. It is Simeon who in compassion warns Mary of the pain she will endure. It is Simeon who gives the church what has come to be a beloved canticle, "Now let your servant depart in peace"—a phrase that was also used at times when slaves were freed. (The first words of the phrase are familiar in the Latin title of the canticle, "Nunc Dimittis.")

But there are parallels between Simeon and Anna, and they are remarkable. Both Simeon and Anna are old. Both are pious, righteous, and devout. Both are looking for the coming of the one who was to become salvation for Israel. Both had their spiritual eyes open to recognize in this child the promised one. However, while Simeon, after praising God for the gift, spoke only to Joseph and Mary, Anna went out and spoke to *"all* who were looking for the redemption of Jerusalem" (Luke 2:38, emphasis added).

41

She, who like other women was confined to the outer courts of the Temple because of her gender, here joins Simeon and breaks forth in wonder. But she goes further! In Luke's Gospel, Anna becomes the first human evangelist, one who tells *others* the good news—others not present at the Temple, other outsiders, others hoping for salvation. With the prophet Isaiah of old, Anna is moved from the wonder of the luminous scene at the Temple to exclaim, "For Zion's sake I will not keep silent" (Isa. 62:1*a*). She has encountered in the child the wonder of the grace of God, the liberating, life-giving, barrier-breaking wonder of God in Christ, before whom there are no gender, age, race, or status walls. She has a voice, and her breaking forth in wonder is heard beyond the Temple's walls, heard by those who had long sat in the darkness of night. Her evangel song is Simeon's song: "These eyes have seen salvation's dawn. . . . This is the savior of the world, the Gentiles' promised light, God's glory dwelling in our midst, the joy of Israel" (from the paraphrase of the words of Simeon in James Quinn, "Song of Simeon," *The Presbyterian Hymnal* [Louisville: Westminster/John Knox, 1990], 603).

Thus Simeon and Anna both proclaim the new reality of the one who will bring salvation for all people. The ones whom society diminishes God exalts. The ones who were once outsiders become the very ones about whom it is said, "You shall be a crown of beauty in the hand of the LORD, and a royal diadem in the hand of your God" (Isa. 62:3).

That is the gospel news this first Sunday after Christmas: In Jesus Christ no one is slave to sin, separated from God by distinctions or limitations of any form. Rather each one is a child of God and heir with Christ through the grace of God (Gal. 4:7).

The church has prized this story and the message it conveys so much that it has used Simeon's peaceful canticle at a critical juncture in its own liturgical life. At the conclusion of the celebration of the Eucharist, the church has traditionally sung, "Now let your servant depart in peace." For the church has recognized that in the breaking of bread, we, like Simeon and Anna, encounter God in Jesus Christ, and hope and grace are born anew. At the table the church meets the one before whom, in the words of John Calvin, all we can do is "break forth in wonder" (John Calvin, *Institutes of Christian Religion*, ed. John McNeill, trans. Ford L. Battles [Philadelphia: Westminster, 1960], 4.17.4, p. 1367).

But the church has done more than contemplate the beauty of God's incarnate grace in the sanctuary or at the table. Throughout history the church has also been compelled to go out, like Anna, taking with it in life and speech the gospel of grace. Like Anna, we are compelled to shine upon the world the fullness of the gospel news of redemption. Following the steps of the old, widowed woman Anna, who out of oppression's grip was silent no longer, we go out to become instruments of redemption, righteousness, and peace. Anna lived out Simeon's song. A freed slave who departed from the holy place in peace, Anna went out in joy, a new woman, a new being, empowered for life, eager to share the grace that she had found.

The invitation this first Sunday after Christmas is the same one proclaimed from Anna's heart long ago. For the child whom Simeon and Anna first extolled is the same child who later gave his life so that salvation could come to all who sit in darkness—so that *all* with Simeon and Anna might break forth in wonder and sing, *"These eyes have seen salvation's dawn."*

SUGGESTIONS FOR WORSHIP

A Litany

[Note: all responses are to be sung in the key of G major, using tunes from the following carols: "Angels We Have Heard on High" (Refrain, first line); "O Little Town of Bethlehem" (fourth stanza, second line); "See Amid the Winter's Snow" (Refrain).]

Creator God,
Earth and sky join the song
the angels sing:

Gloria in Excelsis Deo

Jesus Christ,
You dwelt among us
and we found grace.

Gloria in Excelsis Deo

Holy Spirit,
Your gentle voice assures us
that in Christ we inherit God's riches.

Gloria in Excelsis Deo

Holy Triune God,
when our sins keep us as slaves,

Cast out our sin and enter in,
Be born in us today

When we fail to see you
in the guise of the oppressed,

Cast out our sin and enter in,
Be born in us today

When we are satisfied with
sanctuary rituals
and fail to take salvation's dawn
to the darkness of the world,

Cast out our sin and enter in,
be born in us today

Grace-giving God,
in your coming all women find strength,
all men find gentleness,
all youth find wisdom,
all aged find joy.

As Simeon and Anna of old
recognized and sang your glory,
so lead us to see salvation's dawn,
and break forth in wonder
in witness to the world.

Hail that ever blessed morn, Hail redemptions's happy dawn,
Sing through all Jerusalem: Christ is born in Bethlehem.

(Edward Caswell, "See Amid the Winter's Snow," *The Presbyterian Hymnal* [Louisville: Westminster/John Knox, 1990], 51)

Epiphany

Margaret K. Schwarzer

Isaiah 60:1-7: God proclaims that redemption is dawning in the lives of God's people: "Arise, shine; for your light has come." In the lush vision of the restored Zion which follows, God promises that "[Nations] shall bring gold and frankincense, and shall proclaim the praise of the Lord."

Psalm 72:1-7, 10-14: This psalm prays for God's abundant blessing upon Israel's new king: "May all kings fall down before him, all nations give him service."

Ephesians 3:1-12: Paul reminds his readers that he was sent by God to be a missionary to the Gentiles. The Gentile church is part of God's salvific plan.

Matthew 2:1-12: This scripture tells the story of the Magi's journey. While seeking the Messiah, the Magi are misled by Herod, but they still find Jesus by following the star. After they worship the baby and his mother they are released from Herod's trap by a holy dream.

REFLECTIONS

During the seasons of Christmas and Epiphany, our challenge as preachers is to dig into the truth of the incarnation in such a way that our congregations will grasp the shocking and audacious gift of God-made-flesh. In the midst of our secular and materialistic culture, this is no small task. Because of the yearly repetition of Christ's birth narrative and the Christmas season's focus upon this story, the plot will have been well considered in the past five weeks. It will be hard for the congregation to come to this narrative with fresh enthusiasm or curiosity. Further, some intellectual Christians do not

45

believe that this story has anything to teach them because there is neither historical proof nor archaeological evidence to validate any of its details. Finally, there is no obvious theological tension within this text which requires resolution. This is not one of Paul's letters; this is a story whose content—God's incarnation—is couched in a straightforward and simple narrative. Despite the centrality of this text in our faith, the text's power and importance can be remarkably difficult to convey.

For these reasons, I found myself looking for modern stories of God's love which could jump-start the congregation into a deeper appreciation of God's ancient love for us. In light of our existence on the cusp of the millennium, I considered the Berlin Wall's destruction and South African apartheid's end; a compelling sermon could be preached about love's ability to vanquish the "Herods" of this world. But though I wanted to hold up the power of incarnate love in this sermon, I decided to execute that theme by going another way. I decided to invite the congregation to recognize the power of God's dwelling among us through the realm of the intimate, not the epic. Rather than demonstrate God's salvific action in events of global proportion, I tried to echo the wisdom of the stable, where tenderness and vulnerability are used to reveal the essential aspects of God's identity. As I looked for a chance to communicate God's incarnation, the tender and the whimsical presented themselves as tools for our appreciation of the mystery and grace of Emmanuel.

A SERMON BRIEF

This Gospel scripture invites us to reflect upon Christmas pageants—not just the first pageant, described in Matthew and Luke, where Magi, shepherds, and angels flow in and out of the stable in a loosely structured dance—but the many Christmas pageants that have been staged since. These seasonal pageants invite all of us to playfully engage in the wonder of God-made-flesh.

Do you remember what it was like to be an angel, or a shepherd, or a star for one hour? Remember trying on the costume while your heart tried on an angel's identity, a star's mystery, a shepherd's adventure? All over the globe, for hundreds of years, adults and children have reenacted the incarnation with a Christmas pageant. Whimsy and playfulness are meant to be important parts of Christmas!

We have a splendid pageant on Christmas Eve when some of our children wave a cosmos of stars into the empty space behind our main altar and others take on the role of halo-wearing angels or turban-wearing shepherds, all circling around the virgin and child who are seated at the base of the main altar. Usually a shepherd or two trip on their long tunics, the stars compete to see whose star is the tallest, and at least one angel cries, but the pageant is all the more wonderful because of that. No one acts stiff or artificial; real, little human beings are doing their best to welcome God. But like those of us who are observers, they carry their humanness with them.

Most serious scholars point out that the Gospels' birth narratives have not been substantiated by nonbiblical historical texts. Unlike other portions of the Old and New Testaments, there is no corroboration of any of the details Matthew presents to us in texts of Greek, Roman, Persian, or Aramaic origin. Neither do the birth narratives parallel any first-century Christian writing. So we scientific twentieth-century Christians cannot confirm that these detailed stories of shepherds or Magi actually happened as historical fact.

Yet one look at a Christmas pageant will tell us that the value of these stories is not based upon their factual reality—whatever that may be—but upon the spiritual truths they communicate. Like poetry or music or dance, these stories herald to the world the mystery and wonder of Christ's incarnation. Christ's birth resonates with so much significance that the cosmos itself could not remain neutral, so it produced a star. Christ's birth was so significant that wise astrologers from far-away places journeyed hundreds of miles because they read in heaven's alignment what most of Bethlehem couldn't read in Mary's face. Christ's birth was so significant that ever since those first wise men, men and women have been moved to great lengths to seek God and to celebrate when they found God.

The adoration of the Magi may be the first Bible story most of us learn. I knew it before I went to kindergarten because the basic plot is a simple one: dress up, get a make-believe gift, and hand it over to the baby. My strongest memory of a Christmas pageant comes from the Christmas when I was four. It was a pageant with only three characters, which took place in my parents' living room on a cold December afternoon.

My twin sister, Mary, and I were playing in the living room while my oldest sister, Louise, listened to Beatles records upstairs and my mother cooked in the kitchen. When the doorbell rang and David, a college friend of my sister's, arrived, Mom asked him to wait in the living room while she went to retrieve Louise. To four-year-olds, any adult seemed to be fair game for playing, so Mary and I quickly pressed the unsuspecting guest into service, insisting that he take on the role of Mary, so that we could parade in with our gifts, as the wise men. To his credit, David grumbled only a little when we gave him a blue cocktail dress that had belonged to my grandmother; we insisted he wear it on his head, as a veil. Then the naked plastic baby doll was handed over and David knelt in front of the Christmas tree. Mary and I left the room to make an entrance just as my mother and older sister came down the stairs, so they got back to the living room before we did. What my oldest sister made of her date dressed up like the Virgin Mary, I do not know, but even though I was only four, I think I remember a gasp.

I do know I remember the thick silence in that room immediately preceding our enthusiastic performance. In we went, in my dad's shoes and coats, and we presented our gifts—a stone pillbox and a glass ashtray—to Mary and the baby. Over a decade later, I learned that David was from a conservative Jewish family and had vehement feelings about the Christian calendar's domination of American culture. He'd walked into our house that day and been turned into the overdressed focal point of a faith he didn't believe in and a culture he rejected; but he graciously entered our story anyway.

It has struck me since then that there is something appropriate in a Christmas pageant containing a conservative Jew's generosity to two little Gentile girls. Christ's becoming flesh and dwelling among us is at least as preposterous as a Jewish college man dressing up as the Virgin Mary. Christ's willingness to enter into the vulnerabilities and absurdities of humankind is well paralleled by David's respectful hold on our plastic baby Jesus. What is Christ's love for us like? Christ's love is like the bent body of a Jewish man wearing an old cocktail dress on his head, cradling a naked plastic baby doll. With all its silliness and social tension, that living room pageant points to a core truth about incarnation. God will enter into all the games we play, and seek us while we play them. And God does not enter our games half-heartedly. "For God so loved the world that [God] gave [God's] only son, so that everyone who believes in him may not perish but may have eternal life" (John 3:16).

If many of us now feel too old for the physical playfulness of Christmas pageants, we will still be well served to play them in our imaginations. This year, as in every year, we are invited to decide where we stand in relation to the Christ. Where do you see yourself located in this year's manger scene? Each vantage point has its advantages and drawbacks. Are you drawn to the shepherds abiding in their fields, full of appreciation for open skies, busy with daily tasks, and still ready to make room to seek God? Or are you drawn to the vigor and restlessness of wise men, or the pondering, quiet wisdom of Mary? Perhaps you are a dove, hovering in the rafters, drowsy and comfortable, resting in Christ's presence, or perhaps you are a manger goat this year, vaguely aware that you are in the general vicinity of God, but distracted by the cud you are chewing. If we're lucky, in our life span we will all play many roles. When you recognize your place in this year's manger scene, I invite you to tell at least one person, so you will have a comrade in the playful wisdom most of us took for granted as children.

Of course, if you take me up on my invitation, you will be taking a risk. Some adults might find your story to be so vulnerable that they won't know what to say. Then again, in response to your story, someone might tell you where *they* stand in relation to Christ this Christmas. There's no predicting what grace might provide in such a sacred game. Great wisdom and great peace can come out of tender moments. What is certain is that if we do tell our own story this Christmas, we will also be telling the story of stories afresh. We will be proclaiming that Christ is born and dwells with us. And when his story is set in motion, grace arrives to teach us, and love arrives to heal us. There's no telling what we might discover about God or ourselves in those stories.

When I reflect upon my relationship with Christ this December, I'm making the same choice I made when I was four; the vigor and adventure of the wise men energize me. I need to do some determined searching for God this year. But when I anticipate next year, I already have my eye on Mary and the dreaming wisdom that lets her rest in Christ's presence. For each of us in this Epiphany there is a star to discover, a journey to take, a manger to rest within.

SUGGESTIONS FOR WORSHIP

Call to Worship (adapted from Isaiah 60:1-7)

LEADER: "Arise, shine; for your light has come."
            Lift up your eyes for the grace of God is near us.
PEOPLE: **Holy One, we open our eyes;**
            We lift our voices to you.

LEADER: "Arise, shine; for your light has come."
Open your hearts, for the Prince of Peace is near us.

PEOPLE: **Holy One, we open our hearts;**
We lift our voices to you.

LEADER: "Arise, shine; for your light has come."
Rejoice; the righteousness and mercy of God dwell with us.

PEOPLE: **Holy One, we rejoice;**
We lift our voices to you.

Prayer of Confession

Gracious God, we are a sinful people. Often our hearts are cold and our faith is thin. In the midst of our broken world, our souls shrivel, and our bitterness expands. Refresh our hearts and renew our hopes. Kindle in us the delight and joy you gave us at our birth.

Assurance of Pardon

Hear the good news. We are forgiven and called to new life through Jesus Christ our Lord. Our sins are forgiven in the name of God: maker of love, giver of life, redeemer of all. Amen.

Benediction

May God's light inspire you;
May God's angels guide you;
May God's love protect you.
May Christ, our Emmanuel,
Dwell with you this day and forevermore. Amen.

Baptism of the Lord

Gláucia Vasconcelos Wilkey

Genesis 1:1-5: The first words of the Bible introduce basic concepts in the story of salvation: The themes of water, newness, and beginnings are connected to and depend on the creative presence of the spirit, the *rûach* of God. In this hymn the voice of God is heard as it was at Jesus' baptism. Here that voice calls creation "good"; later it calls the baptized servant "beloved." The beginning of our biblical history is already gospel news.

Psalm 29: A wondrous, three-stanza psalm of praise to the God of the waters, both of creation and of destruction. Inviting the heavenly beings to praise God, the psalmist points to the mighty power of the Spirit with images that are as evocative and powerful as a flood. The voice that calls forth the storms is the voice that called forth life out of the watery chaos at creation. The wonderful juxtaposition of images of water and fire (v. 7) surely reminded Israel of the Elijah event (the contest between Baal and Israel's God). In the fourth century C.E. Gregory of Nyssa made the connection between fire and baptism: "When Elijah had thrice poured water upon the cleft wood, he kindled at his prayer the fire from out the water." After the storms, the voice above the floods speaks of peace, the promise that the stormiest waters cannot quench the peace-giving presence of God.

Acts 19:1-7: Two profound and disturbing questions are posed to early Christians and to today's church. What do the speech-acts of baptism imply? What are the theological groundings and what are the ethical consequences of baptism? As countless liturgical theologians have claimed, this passage urges the church to a more faithful understanding of both the theology and the praxis of the sacrament in worship and life. The connections between the life-giving Spirit, the

. . .

. . .

preached word, and the enacted word as disclosed in worship must also result in life patterned after the ways of Jesus. In an age during which many search for worship practices that imitate the age of entertainment, Paul reminds us that it is the Spirit that gives renewal and life to worship. In an age in which religious values are spoken but not lived, Paul calls the church to faithfulness to its baptismal anointing, an anointing that empowers for prophetic ministry.

Mark 1:4-11: Mark's account of Jesus' baptism is stark in comparison to the other Gospels. Mark focuses strongly on the issue of baptism as identity-giving, an event that is the beginning of a revelatory process that connects Jesus with the past (roots) and the present (mission). The opening of the heavens clearly indicates the presence of the glory of God (of which Psalm 29 also speaks). The spirit of grace cascades over Jesus in the gentle, embracing, and empowering words "beloved" and "son" (words probably already familiar to Jesus, since they come from Psalm 2). Mark's use of the words is significant in that they are repeated at two other significant events in Jesus' life: his transfiguration (ch. 9) and his crucifixion (ch. 14). The identity of the baptized is that of "servant" (as in the "suffering servant" of Isaiah). Baptism shapes the identity of and gives direction to the life of the beloved.

REFLECTIONS

"Baptism of the Lord" is a day on which we both remember Christ's baptism, and celebrate our own. As a person charged with worship education in my denomination, I have an ongoing passion for lifting up and deepening understanding regarding this often undervalued sacrament in our church's life. However, I also want to do so in a way that moves beyond didacticism and that helps evoke anew the power of this sacrament in all its symbolic mystery. By calling to memory my own experiences of baptism as a child in Brazil, I hope to help others remember and deepen their own biblical, theological, and existential understanding of this holy act.

A SERMON BRIEF

The River at the Gathering Place

It was an amazing place, that gathering place in my childhood. It all began when my father was serving as an itinerant preacher. The congregation was made up of a number of farming families in a remote corner of the state where I was born, in the heartland of Brazil. Once a year, instead of getting together in small groups for worship as they ordinarily did, the people came to one place, a slice of one of the farms in the area.

The first year we met there, someone drew a sign at the gated entrance that read simply, "Ponto de Encontro," Portuguese for "Point of Encounter," or "The Gathering Place." It was many years before I would value that name as much as I do today.

A few months before our first meeting, when the leaders were thinking about a site for that gathering, the following criteria were established: (1) the gathering place had to be easily accessible to all; (2) the gathering place had to be by a clean, living stream of water, near its source, and (3) the gathering place had to have plenty of trees, preferably mango trees. Those were the requirements!

Why a clean, living stream near its source? Basic survival. No, not for drinking water only. This stream also provided for the spiritual needs of the community. For on Sunday, the final day at the gathering place, baptism was celebrated. Every year, on the Sunday we celebrate today, Baptism of the Lord, the people gathered by that stream and reveled in living out the hymn that quickly became the theme song of that place: "Shall We Gather at the River."

The place where we met for worship was called "the shed." It was just that, a rough shed. The people sat on even rougher benches. First and foremost it was our sanctuary, but it also served a host of other functions. We all lived there for eight glorious days, and I loved that place! Every year for five years of my life that place was as new as new creation. And we certainly called it good.

In that river in that gathering place we quenched our physical and our spiritual thirst. We bathed our bodies and we cleansed our souls, we splashed and played, we children grew together, and the water was the beginning and the center of it all. It was a new creation every year, that Sunday was. Every year that Sunday was new and fresh and glorious. We called the day "good" and we sang "Shall We Gather at the River."

53

There is more to the story. The rough shed had a unique design: the water flowed *through* it. On the east side of the interior stood the pulpit; and in front of it, a simple, unadorned table. Across the stream, on the west side, were the seats. All the furnishings were hewn out of trees on the property. To get from west to east, you had to cross the stream.

The people pitched their tents south of the sanctuary. And since the source of the water was north of the gathering place on a gently sloping hill, it looked from our tent site as if the water literally flowed from the sanctuary (as in Ezekiel 47 and Revelation 22). It was many years before I could name the reasons for that design or relate it to biblical imagery, theology, eschatology, or anything else. All I knew as a young girl was that we gathered on the week of the Baptism of the Lord, we heard Jesus' own baptismal story retold, and, year after year, we saw it reenacted. All I knew then was that during that particular week I was going to be with friends in that wonderful place—and that we loved to sing "Shall We Gather at the River."

There is even more to the story. You heard me say the farmers wanted to build the place near mango trees. In this property there was a large mango grove. Why mango trees? For one thing, they are large trees, rich in foliage, and we could hide from the blistering sun underneath their rich canopy. We could also hang our hammocks there. And we could, of course, eat the beautiful fruit, one of creation's good things.

Nutritionists tell us that mangos are good for us. The fruit is rich in fiber and lots of vitamins and minerals that are essential for our survival. And it is delightfully tasty. In fact, you have not had a good, juicy, golden, heavenly tasting fruit unless you have eaten a Brazilian mango taken fresh from the tree. There is more: the leaves are used for a delicious tea, with medicinal qualities. And the leaves can also be cooked and pressed and used as balm for wounds. Those leaves could indeed serve for the healing of the community. It was many years before I could name the reasons for trees by the water in the gathering place, or to relate the fruits or the leaves of the trees to biblical imagery, to the goodness of God's creation, to theology, eschatology, or anything else.

I could not then ascribe the warmth and love and the power of the place to the very presence of the spirit of God in the community, calling it, and me, "Beloved." And I certainly did not think much then about the ways in which my life outside the gathering place should portray my week by the river. All I knew as a young girl was that I

looked forward to the week of the Baptism of the Lord, fc
we would be with friends in that wonderful, warm, embracing ɡᵤ
ering place. And I knew we called the place "good," and that there we
would be singing "Shall We Gather at the River."

But as we heard the story of the baptism of Jesus year after year, it
finally dawned on me: if baptism for Jesus implied changing the
world, reordering its values—rich made poor, poor made rich, well-fed
made hungry, hungry made satisfied, blind made to see, the wise made
foolish, women receiving honor, and children seen as role models for the
world—then there must be more to baptism than I glimpsed in my
childhood, however rich that experience had been. If baptism for Jesus
Christ meant the coming of the Spirit, empowering him for gracious
living, then there must be something more to baptism than the beauty of the water and the joy of friends at the gathering place.

Remember the sign at the entrance gate? As we came in we read the
words "The Gathering Place." Someone, however, scribbled two words
on the *back* of that sign. When we left the place of new creation the
message we received sent us out into the world in the manner of Jesus
Christ. For the gate to the world read, "Servants' Entrance."

As the gathering place and the baptism of Jesus grew in meaning to
the woman I came to be, I also came to see that the water of the river
is the womb of rebirth, the font of identity for the people of God. I
now know that to be drenched with that water is to be immersed in a
death like Christ's: death to the world's values, which are at odds with
God's ways of justice and grace for all, so that we can be born to a new
way of living. Just as baptism was for Jesus the beginning of a new life
for a parched world, so my baptism, like Christ's, must not end at the
font. It must be carried out for the sake of the world—so that, indeed,
baptism and ethics merge and flow together.

I now know that being baptized means immersion into resurrection, the new creation lived and promised by Jesus Christ. It does
mean new life, life inaugurated by the one baptized by John and
anointed by the Spirit. And I now see that the child I was, beloved of
God, could do much more than sing a beautiful song in a beautiful
place. She too, anointed by the Spirit, could go out into the river of
need in the world in the name of the beloved servant baptized in the
river Jordan.

Servants of Christ, "Shall we gather at the river?"

SUGGESTIONS FOR WORSHIP

A Baptismal Litany

Creator God,
your voice brought forth life
out of the watery chaos.
We praise you, O God.

Jesus Christ,
your baptism opened in us
life-giving streams.
We praise you, O Christ.

Holy Spirit,
in baptism you anoint us
and fire our souls with power.
We praise you, O Spirit.

Holy triune God,
where our sins dry us up,
flood us with your grace.
Have mercy on us.

When we forget
who we are,
once more call us "Beloved."
Have mercy on us.

When we fail
to be water for the thirsty,
flood us with the spirit of Christ.
Have mercy on us.

Eternal God,
fount of mercy,
in the baptism of Jesus
you called him "Beloved."
Anointed by the Spirit,
Jesus was empowered for living.
Keep us faithful by the power of your spirit,
that we may live as the people of the water,
the font where we heard you naming *us*,
and calling *us* "Beloved."
Through Jesus Christ our Lord. **Amen.**

Transfiguration Sunday

Joan Dennehy

---

2 Kings 2:1-12: Elisha yearns to be recognized as the spiritual heir of his teacher, Elijah, who ascends to heaven.

Psalm 50:1-6: God is not the silent creator but shines forth and summons creation.

2 Corinthians 4:3-6: We call one another to faith, not letting weariness defeat us, but strengthened by beliefs held deep in our hearts.

Mark 9:2-9: In a moment of highest mystery, Jesus is glimpsed as God with us, one worth listening to.

REFLECTIONS

Is the transfiguration of Jesus historically true? Did Peter have some kind of vision? Is this someone's account of a resurrection appearance, projected back into the narrative of the Galilean ministry? Or is it pure symbolism—a way to show Jesus full of the glory of God? There are problems with each of those interpretations; none of them can be accepted to the exclusion of the rest. But clearly, something very significant happened.

Mark's version is the most sparse. This is intuitive, experiential material, and even though it is followed by cognitive, rational material, it is fitting to honor the former. I don't think the disciples are intellectually confused here. They are mystified and full of awe. All their senses are stimulated. This is about firsthand faith. For all of us, and perhaps especially for women, it is important not to settle for secondhand faith. Each of us is God's vessel of revelation, both unique and unitive.

A SERMON BRIEF

In a story I once read, a large stone rolled across the river one night and took up residence on the other side of the water. The people did not know how it happened that a stone had crossed the river. One curious man decided to sleep on the stone in order to learn its mysteries. Every night he climbed on the stone and went to sleep. Every morning he found himself thrown off, lying instead on the ground. And so it is that we are thrown back to earth from our night journeys into mystery—waking daily at the feet of creation in ordinary time.

Once upon a time there was no time, and Jesus, Peter, John, and James climbed up and down a rock. By our standards here in the northwest, it was barely a hill, about 1,800 feet above sea level. From a distance it looked like a woman's breast. I was taught that this story, different from the rest of Mark's Gospel, is so cloaked in uncertainty that all I could do was probe around its edges. The older I've gotten the more audacious I've become. Like the man who doggedly climbed on the stone, I want more out of this mystery. There is a hunger in me for God's voice in sacred time. There is the weight of a thousand veils around my soul and I would do my part to loosen them.

This wasn't the first time that James, Peter, and John had gone off alone with Jesus. Busy one afternoon with crowd control, they saw him divert his attention to a grieving father. In the remarkable way that Jesus could pour love over fear, they saw in that father's eyes the peace of their teacher. *Only have faith,* he was saying as he beckoned the three of them to follow. Oh, my. Those three words took up much more pondering space inside these disciples than ever they did on lip or pen.

On that same day, their teacher took them into the bedroom of a child, as good as dead. Along with her mother and father, they saw that child quicken. As they left, faces shining, you could hear the pots rattling in the kitchen. *Bread of life* breathes the mother, doors and passageways opening within her.

On a subsequent day, on a mountain alone with Jesus, the disciples saw Jesus catch fire from within. No, not fire: glory! They saw him with prophets as good as dead, as if time were nothing but a veil to be parted and stepped through. They heard a voice with parts of themselves better equipped to hear than ears. Then the voice rolled itself up and went quiet. On that day, James, Peter, and John were called away from longing into experience. It was something they remembered. But how? "It happened this way," John said. "He was singing . . . " James heard weeping as if Jesus were raindrops falling on the land. Peter felt the earth tremble. "Yes, it was wonderful," they agreed.

I heard about a woman who approached a street corner one day, noticing a sudden dark deadness in the sky. Large clouds formed. Wind blew. From behind the darkest cloud emerged a bright light. With held breath she watched liquid gold pour from the light. She watched the form of Jesus appear. She stared and waited. She could hear and feel the words he said: *Be in communion with me.* Then light, color, body, and cloud disappeared.

Do you believe this can happen? I do not choose to be caustic, cynical, or despairing. The history of Christianity reveals a willingness among Christians to derive sustenance from the experience of others. And I do. It opens me. It's not that I think the spiritual clothing of one person can be worn by another. But symbolically I do climb to the top of the mountain seeking to touch the energy of the divine, to see further than I have ever seen before. I want to receive as much of God as I am given. Is not the aim of life to be divinely awake?

Toward the end of his life, Carl Jung was asked if he believed in God. After a long pause, he answered, "I don't believe, I know. I know." I need this story. Without the story of a transfigured Jesus glimpsed by others like me I would be less open, less trusting of the spiritual insights revealed to me. I would be less confident to say *I know.*

It is interesting that the word *revelation* literally means "to veil again." The world of the soul is glimpsed through the opening of a veil that closes again. When we stand in those places where the veils part it is not like standing in a hospital operating room. It is not a place of severe and insistent light. In those clouded places near heaven the light is like that of a candle. There is shadow and color in every candle flame. It befriends the darkness, hospitable to what is reserved and hidden. It prompts the imagination into activity.

How cruel it is when others abuse our capacity for imagination. George remembers a childhood drawing of an island with a palm tree and a sun dropping below the horizon. He remembers thinking, *This is good, this must be what an island really looks like.* Of course he had never seen an island or a palm tree, and soon the teacher was by his desk saying, "That's not how you draw palm trees." With a few strokes of her pen she made his trees look proper. He never drew again.

The power to imagine is the foundation of all art and religion. Lots of people are only too willing to tell us what God is like so that we stop imagining. We come to worship not to be told what God is like, but to be in the presence of God; and I have seen your faces when that happens. You are more fully yourselves than at any other time.

Every time Jesus caught a glimpse of God he became stronger, wiser, kinder, and more daring. All the way to Good Friday's mountain and the night a large stone rolled to the other side of the water.

SUGGESTIONS FOR WORSHIP

Call to Worship

LEADER: The silence is deep. We bring ourselves to God whose joy it is to be with us.

ALL: **We prepare ourselves to listen so that the Holy Spirit may teach us the truth about God. What we see and hear is a gift.**

Prayer of Confession

O Mystery, how many times have you revealed yourself and we have been distracted? How many times have we searched for you too intensely, trying to solve riddles and control the unknown? The more we ponder it the more we know it is true. If you are to shape our life, if your ways are to guide our steps, then we must know that you, beyond name and beyond form, touch us and others in ways that go beyond understanding. Who knows where you will show up next? You are gift beyond measure.

Assurance of Pardon

The glory of Christ, who is the image of God, shines from the rising of the sun to its setting. The beloved has come and will not keep silent.

Benediction

May God be gladness in your heart and on your face to light a path in a beautiful and dangerous world. You are blessed this day and always.

Ash Wednesday

Rhonda VanDyke Colby

Joel 2:1-2, 12-17: Rend your hearts and not your garments. Return to God.

Psalm 51:1-17: A prayer for mercy and forgiveness. Sin is against God.

2 Corinthians 5:20b–6:10: Be reconciled to God.

Matthew 6:1-6, 16-21: Giving to the needy and appropriate fasting. Secret sacrifices are seen by God.

REFLECTIONS

A Lenten dilemma: How do you talk about sin and sacrifice without the congregation tuning out immediately? This question caused me to look for new ways to address these Lenten themes.

Sacrifice is letting go. Psalm 51 and Matthew 6 deal with the kinds of sacrifice that please God. Sin is brokenness, debt, transgressions—all "tune out" words. However, sin is also "stuckness." It is like a quicksand pit that slowly sucks the abundant life out of us. It causes a kind of paralysis of powerlessness. The way out of the stuckness is not by showy battles against evil any more than the appropriate way to give to the needy or to fast is by "showiness." The way out of the paralysis of powerlessness over sin is, as the recovery movements have shown us, *admitting* powerlessness. This admission of powerlessness and complete release is beautifully expressed in Psalm 51. The phrase "broken and contrite heart" calls to mind a child caught doing something wrong and desiring to make it right even if it means letting go of something precious. That is the nature of surrender, confession, and release.

61

A SERMON BRIEF

Getting Unstuck

"Mommy, I'm stuck." That's the way the adventure began. Three-year-old Crystal came to her mother holding in one hand her great grandmother's vase. The other hand couldn't be seen. It was stuck inside the vase.

Crystal's mother tried to move quickly without panicking, because the vase was valuable to her. Holding the vase and her little girl, she carried Crystal to the kitchen sink. She used warm soapy water to try to loosen the toddler's hand, which was indeed stuck. When soap didn't work she reached for the butter. While greasing her child's wrist like a cake pan she asked the obvious "mother question." "How in the world did you do this?" Crystal explained that she dropped candy down into the vase to see if she could still see it when it was at the very bottom. She couldn't. When she reached in for her candy she couldn't get her hand back out.

The more time went on the more serious the whole situation became. Mother called grandmother to come over and help assess the situation. A neighbor suggested Vaseline. The apartment manager got the WD40. Still no luck. It seemed like the only way to get the child's hand out was to break the heirloom.

Grandma arrived with her calming presence and went over to Crystal, who was very upset and still very stuck. "Sweetheart," she said gently, "Mommy says you reached in the vase for candy. Is that right?"

"Mmm hmm," the child whimpered, still breathless from crying.

"Honey, tell grandma the truth now. Do you still have a hold of that candy?"

"Mmm hmm," she sobbed.

The grandmother patted her back to comfort her. "Let it go, child. Let it go."

The vase slipped off as smooth as silk.

Ash Wednesday begins the season of Lent when we remember that Jesus took forty days in the wilderness for prayer and contemplation. It is traditionally a time when we take a serious look at our lives. We look long and hard at ourselves and discover some things we don't like. It's time for some self-assessment. It's time for some change.

Here at the beginning of Lent is Ash Wednesday. It's the one day of the year when we remember that we came from dust and that we will return to dust. We recognize that none of us is invincible; none is immortal; we all will die. It is a day when we recognize that each day, each moment is a gift and not to be wasted.

But we *are* wasting it. To one degree or another we are all wasting the precious abundant life God has given us. We are stuck. At some time along the way we put ourselves somewhere we shouldn't have been. Maybe we knew ahead of time that what we were doing was wrong, that it was sin. Or maybe we stumbled into the situation in innocence. Whatever the case, we got ourselves stuck and we don't know how to get out.

Can you think of when it happened? Can you remember when you first started the habit? Do you remember when you first started to use the drug or when you first got hooked on the grudge—that gripping resentment you have for that person? Do you remember when you let shame and guilt start running your life? Do you remember when you got stuck?

It may not have seemed like such a big deal at first. When the little girl first stuck her hand in the vase it didn't feel very big or heavy. But after an afternoon of carrying it around and trying to be rid of it, it got to be quite a burden.

Some of us are carrying around some burdens that are much larger than an old vase. They don't take just one hand to hold. Our burdens are the big two-handed kind: the kind you carry in your arms and across your back and around your neck. The longer the burden is there the heavier it gets, the more difficult it is to budge. We start looking down instead of up. We get to where we can only see where we are; we can't see where we're going. We are burdened and we are stuck.

There was a time when Jesus was burdened. He carried the burden of a beam on his back. His burden required both hands. The hands that carried the cross bore the wounds. His head was bowed low when he prayed that the cup might pass from him. It was bowed low when he carried the cross. It hung low when he died on the cross. But when Friday sorrow turned to Easter joy our burdens were no more. You see, if Jesus Christ was powerful enough not to be stuck in the grave, then there is nothing in this life that can keep us stuck. We are an unstuck people, free in Jesus Christ!

You may ask, "If that is so, if I am free, then why do I still *feel* so stuck? Why do I let things take hold of me? What can I do to experience the freedom that is mine in Christ Jesus?" If you listen ever so closely you can hear Christ whispering like a loving grandma, "Let it go, child. Let it go." Even if your stuckness is so old you can't remember its name, let it go, child, let it go.

Whatever it is—that favorite sin, that pet worry, that sweet habit that has you stuck—if you release it, you can be free. But if you're too greedy or too scared to let it go, you may go around the rest of your life with a jar on your hand or a monkey on your back or a knot in your gut. Christ is urging you to let it go. Open your fists from their death grip so you can open your hands to Christ.

We each have our pet sins, our heaviest burdens that we need to release and be released from if we are to follow Christ with abandon and joy. Write that burden on the strip of paper you have been given. If you can't write it, imagine it imprinted on the paper. Put it in your fist—really tightly. Silently tell God about that burden. Describe how it has you stuck. Express what the stuckness feels like—how it is exhausting and agonizingly familiar and how you can't remember what it feels like to be unstuck. And ask God through Jesus Christ to help you release it, let it go. When you have prayed that prayer bring your tight-fistedness to the cross and release it so that you can experience freedom. When you let it go from your hand you are symbolically giving it to God to dispose of it permanently.

People always talk about giving up something for Lent. They give up chocolate or bubble gum or soap operas or the sports page. I'm suggesting to you that you give up something more significant than that. I'm suggesting that you give up whatever it is that has a hold on you and keeps you from joyfully and abundantly following Jesus Christ. Give it up for Lent. Let it go, child. Let it go.

SUGGESTIONS FOR WORSHIP

Call to Worship

LEADER: We enter the season of Lent wounded.
PEOPLE: Wounded too deeply to utter a sound. And we stand pressing our hand to the pain.
LEADER: And God comes to us saying, "Show me your wound."
PEOPLE: "No. It's fine. I'm OK."
LEADER: "No. You're not. Show me where you are hurting."
PEOPLE: "No. I can't let go. It hurts."

LEADER:	"I love you. I can heal you. I will restore you."
PEOPLE:	**And we ease our hand away.**
LEADER:	God comes with gentle ointments and soothing balms.
PEOPLE:	**And we cry from the relief of our pain, but we are afraid of being scarred.**
LEADER:	"Not scarred, but shaped," God answers our fears. "Shaped differently from all others, and your new shape will show new things."
PEOPLE:	**God, we give you our tears: tears from loss, from anger, from shame. We give you tears that run silently from our eyes, tears that are so old they no longer have names. We cry from loneliness, from death, from life.**
LEADER:	"And I hear you. I will answer you. I will smooth my hand over your cheek. I will catch your tears and place them in a jar to one day pour them out upon you in joy and forgiveness. You will be restored. You will be set free."
	(Written by Crystal Sygeel-Lystlund for Good Shepherd United Methodist Church, Richmond, Virginia. Used by permission)

Act of Confession and Assurance of Pardon

As people come forward, white-knuckled and tight-fisted, and release the contents of their hands, make the sign of the cross on their palms while holding their hands and saying, "In the name of Jesus Christ you are forgiven." Grant to them the feeling of forgiveness in their hands where moments before their fingernails were making imprints.

Psalm 51 also serves as an eloquently honest prayer for people who long to be unstuck. It can easily be prayed responsively.

Benediction

You have loosened your grip and let it go. What are you left with? Two open hands! Go forth to use your hands to build up and to comfort, to support and to embrace, to soothe and to shake loose. And may our Grandmotherly God whisper wisdom, guidance, and peace to us all.

First Sunday in Lent

Joan Delaplane, O.P.

Genesis 9:8-17: The rainbow becomes the covenantal symbol between God and all creation.

Psalm 25:1-10: A prayer asking that we will be taught God's ways.

1 Peter 3:18-22: As God saved Noah, so, too, by the life, death, and resurrection of Jesus, we are saved in our baptism.

Mark 1:9-15: Jesus is baptized; the Spirit drives him to the desert. After forty days he begins to preach the good news in Galilee.

REFLECTIONS

At the heart of sin is the refusal to be who we are. From Adam and Eve on, there has been within humankind a desire to be God instead of beloved of God. We also have difficulty believing that we imperfect creatures can be or are loved. Many women, especially, struggle with a sense of incompleteness, incompetence, inferiority. No matter how bright and beautiful, educated and gifted, there is a struggle to believe in oneself and to claim and use one's gifts fully. This struggle of Jesus in the desert to understand the depths of the words he heard at his baptism and their ramifications for his life can help every Christian focus anew this Lent.

A SERMON BRIEF

Many characteristics stand out for the man Jesus from Nazareth: person of integrity, courage, and compassion; respecter of persons and creation; teacher of the law and the prophets. But one particular characteristic has impressed me for years. This Jesus knew who he was! And I mean, really knew who he was. Beyond such customary identifiers as lineage (son of Mary and Joseph), hometown (Nazareth), and occupation (carpenter), Jesus, at the core of his being, knew himself to be God's beloved son. He had heard that truth spoken from the heavens at his baptism. Driven by the Spirit, he went out to the desert for forty days and nights to struggle with the ramifications of this identity.

And what did it mean for Jesus to be God's beloved son? Did it mean that God would protect him from all harm? That God would show divine power through him for all to see? That God would gift him in extraordinary ways? On the contrary, Jesus' long, hard wrestling surfaced this truth: that as beloved son he was to make known to all people God's extravagant love. He was to give utterance with his lips and his life that God's reign had begun in him. The time of salvation, of shalom, the time when "justice and peace shall kiss" was present in Jesus. And what Jesus could be assured of was this: as beloved son, God's steadfast love would always be present to him. Nothing and no one could alter that reality.

From Adam and Eve, to Cain and Abel, to the tower of Babel, humankind has had a difficult time with identity. Always and everywhere, it seems, lurks the primal sin of our wanting to be God. If we can't be God, at least we hope to find our worth in "being over" someone else: White over Black; man over woman; one person's gifts over another's; rich over poor; First World over Third World. We "miss the mark," and greed, envy, jealousy, prejudice, hatred, lust, anger take hold. Sin is what it's called!

A few years ago I attended the Ash Wednesday service at the Roman Catholic Cathedral in Oakland, California. As part of the ritual, we were directed to turn to the person coming down the aisle next to us, and with ashes to make the sign of the cross on the person's forehead. It was assumed, I believe, that the usual statement would be made: that is, "Remember you are dust and into dust you shall return," or its alternate, "Repent, and believe the good news!" An elderly African American woman was next to me. When it came time for my anointing she looked me in the eye, took a massive thumb-full of ashes, crossed me generously, and said in a loud, clear voice: "Trust God!"

Every Lent since then, I have taken that challenge as being at the heart of what the season of repentance is about: Trust that I am God's beloved daughter and, like Jesus, live out of that truth each day! Through the waters of baptism, I have been claimed as God's own.

None of the flattery of others makes me any better than I am before God; none of the lies, hatred, or disparaging remarks of others makes me any worse.

Jesus did not let outside forces name him. Some wanted to crown him king; others called him Beelzebub. But Jesus' identity was rooted in the truth that he heard at his baptism. He was beloved of God, and that truth freed him to be Jesus!

Our refusal to trust our baptismal identity and to live out of that truth lies at the center of much that gets out of focus and leads to sin in our lives. Yet to claim our dignity and worth as being based solely in God's gratuitous gift of love calls for a humility that is very countercultural today. Certainly our propensity for independence and autonomy get in the way. So do those societal messages, often communicated through the media, that hold up for us a different measuring rod for human dignity and worth: one marked by possessions, prestige, power, beauty, or intelligence. And yet we also know that many among us who have obtained these so-called "marks of dignity" still find within an emptiness, a hunger, a searching that asks, "Is this all there is?"

I wonder: What would happen each morning if, as the waters in the shower come down upon each Christian, each one would recall the waters of baptism by which she or he has been claimed by God? What if each heard anew, at the start of each new day, "You are my beloved daughter. You are my beloved son"? And what if each Christian then and there responded, "Lord, grant me the grace to let every thought, word, and action of this day be worthy of my identity as your child"? No longer would the approval of others or fear of disapproval be a motivating force. No longer would the false gods hold such a strong appeal.

As Christians, we are called to reflect daily on whether or not we are living the way. It is easy to get sidetracked. The shortcuts or detours often hold appeal: Leisure Lane, Dynamic Power Drive, Pleasure Path, Security Street. They are all downhill and look like fun, especially when compared to the arduous climb of the way.

Yet the call of the church this Lenten season summons us to an intense communal look at who we are as baptized, where we are going, how we are getting there. Stop! Examine the road map of the Gospels. If we have made a detour, it is time to turn, come back to the way, the truth, the life. The faithful God of the covenant continues to pursue us and longs to bring each one to wholeness, holiness, and happiness as God's own beloved daughter or son.

SUGGESTIONS FOR WORSHIP

Call to Worship

LEADER: Who is fit to climb God's mountain
            and stand in that holy place?

**PEOPLE: Whoever has integrity:
            not chasing shadows, not living lies.**

LEADER: God will bless them,
            their savior will bring justice.

**PEOPLE: They long to see the Lord,
            they seek the face of Jacob's God.**

LEADER: Stretch toward heaven, you gates.
            Open high and wide,
            let the glorious sovereign enter.

PEOPLE: Who is this splendid ruler?

LEADER: The Lord of power and might,
            the conqueror of chaos.
            This splendid ruler is God.

Prayer of Confession

O faithful God of the covenant, we have often turned a deaf ear to your word of love, a hardened heart to our brothers and sisters, a blind eye to the needy in our midst. We have not been faithful to our baptismal covenant, nor walked the way as we promised. According to your steadfast love and your goodness remember us, and have mercy on us, O Lord.

Assurance of Pardon

" 'Come now, let us reason together,' says the LORD. 'Though your sins are like scarlet, they shall be as white as snow; though they are red as crimson, they shall be like wool' " (Isa. 1:18 NIV). People of God, trust now in God's saving word of forgiveness.

Benediction

You are God's work of art, created in Christ Jesus to live the good life as from the beginning God intended you to live it. Go, therefore, confident in God's faithful and steadfast love for you, and be that loving presence in this world.

Second Sunday in Lent

Linda McKinnish Bridges

Genesis 17:1-7, 15-16: The covenant between God, Abraham, and Sarah inaugurates a new beginning, which requires a name change, introduces hope for future generations, and implies a new relationship with God.

Psalm 22:23-31: Praise God for the promise, which not only engenders hope for many, many descendants, but also declares that future generations will be told about the Lord: "Proclaim his deliverance to a people yet unborn."

Romans 4:13-25: The promise made to Abraham does not depend on things that can be seen or touched but rests entirely on "faithing"—God's faith in Abraham and Sarah's faithfulness to their belief that God is faithful.

Mark 8:31-38: God's faithfulness, as revealed in the passion story of Jesus Christ, is not based on what can be seen or not seen by the disciple Peter, who initially demands to know Jesus in glorious, worldly power rather than in quiet, spiritual suffering.

REFLECTIONS

We are blessed or cursed with the desire to know that somehow the events of the present are linked to the future. Women, in particular, like to see life as a tapestry, where various threads of different colors, no matter their texture or design, blend together in one beautiful piece of art. People who like goal setting and details ("J" types on the Myers-Briggs inventory) are those who want to see the end from the beginning in bold, highlighted form on their calendars—from the family calendar on the refrigerator to the professional planner resting neatly in their purse or pocket. We want to know that what happens today will relate to what goes on tomorrow. Connecting chronological dots gives us security and peace of mind.

Consequently, we desire to have children in what psychologists call our "generative phase" so that we can ensure that our present will live on into the future through the life of a child. We create a new business or establish a new educational institution so that life will go on beyond the span of our own ideas. We organize our financial resources into wills and trusts so that our money will have a life beyond our own. We plant oak trees in the backyard, which will outlive all those people who live in the house. It makes us feel good, meets some deep human need, gives us a sense of power and control to know that decisions made today will affect the world tomorrow.

The great, haunting question of these lectionary texts, however, is this: How can we know with certainty that we or our investments will live on into the future? When there are no other trees growing in the backyard, how can we be assured that the oak sapling we just planted will make it even into the next decade? If we have been told that we cannot have children, how do we know that our contribution to the world will have any meaning at all? If we cannot even pay the bills this month, how do we really know that our financial resources will have a future life beyond our tattered checkbook?

As I preach this sermon, I want to try to communicate what Abraham and Sarah were feeling *before* and *after* God verbalized the covenant (Gen. 17). It is not just a feeling of biological barrenness, of empty wombs and quiet playrooms, where they feel that life will cease at their death. Peter's existential dilemma has nothing to do with empty wombs or rooms, but the same lack of congruence appears (Mark 8:31-38). Peter must consider how the gloriously alive teacher, who is confident of self and God, would possibly be positioned in the future on a cross to suffer and die. The chronological dots do not appear to be connected. Spiritual barrenness occurs when our life of faith cannot be imagined beyond what we see in this present moment. Peter, who has the future already mapped out, realizes that he must refigure the chronological dots between the present and future. He desperately struggles with the idea that present suffering could be connected to future glory. To Peter, the dots do not seem to connect. In God's eyes, however, there is connection between past, present, and future.

A SERMON BRIEF

Recently I met my great-grandmother Alice Whiteside McKinnish Smith. I met her not in a seance or mystical dream, but in an old family trunk, long stored in the shed off the barn. I was privy to her world when I opened her trunk, a grand place for personal introductions to the early 1900s and my great grandmother Alice. As far as I could tell no one had disturbed it since she lovingly placed her belongings in the leather travel trunk for safekeeping.

In this wonderful storehouse of treasures I found an old black leather purse still guarding her snuff box and holding her birch tree toothbrush for appropriate dental hygiene; a memory box filled with trinkets, childhood toys, tie tacks and selected jewelry pieces; and piles and piles of letters, some tied with string and cloth bindings, written in beautiful penmanship, some on thick manuscript paper, others on scraps of paper, all revealing their value to the collector and the personality of the writers. The bottom of the trunk was filled with old, frayed prayer books and hymnals, with personal prayers written on cardboard, scraps of paper, blank places in newspaper print, scrap grocery lists, and farming inventory sheets. I had discovered a treasure; I had met my great grandmother. In the guarded safety of this family trunk were stories that traveled back in time as far as 1869: her marriage to James H. McKinnish, correspondence to and from her sons, news of current events clipped from magazines and newspapers, and her deep, deep, inner life of prayer.

Alice was a lady of words in a family of wordsmiths. Her brother owned a publishing firm in downtown Asheville, and her sister, Cordie Bridgewater, wrote published hymns. Alice, however, used her words to write to her family and to her God. And those words described her life to me a century later as I read them from the trunk. Her worn music books spoke of her love for song. Her carefully clipped current events from magazines and papers revealed an awareness of events in the world beyond her world of family and farm. Bank account statements and war ration books showed a life of frugality and simplicity. Her prayers, however, revealed her inner soul. Prayers, some short and some long, revealed a daily life of prayer punctuated by morning invocations and nightly benedictions. She would write a prayer, then date the paper as if she and God had made some kind of covenant that very moment in heavenly conversation.

Her prayers, written on scraps of paper, backs of cardboard boxes, and her correspondence with her adult children revealed her piety and her great disappointments. Her eldest son Oscar left home early and then as a middle-aged man, living many miles from the home place, committed suicide. Arthur left his mother Alice, traveled, wrote home faithfully, and then simply disappeared. No one ever knew of his death or his life after he stopped writing his mother. Edward never married, reveled in life without faith, and later joined the army as a way of serving time for a criminal offense. Daughter Irene was hostile to Christianity until the later years of her life. Alice's youngest son, Loyd, my grandfather, was always opposed to matters of faith, including church and church leaders, even including his preacher son, my father.

Her words of prayer spoke of a relationship with God that did not depend on the present circumstances. She wrote a prayer, labeled "Special Prayer," on an empty space in the side column of a newspaper clipping and then placed it in her Bible: "Father in each thought and word and act of this day, let me be following Thy purpose for my life." She copied this prayer from the newspaper: "Not for the mighty world, O Lord, tonight, Nations and kingdoms in their fearful might—Let me be glad the kettle gently sings, Let me be thankful for the little things. Thankful for simple food and supper spread, Thankful for shelter and a warm, clean bed."

Her children were devoted to her but not devout to her God. She wrote prayers on their behalf and sent letters outlining the plan of salvation to her wayward sons thousands of miles away. She had outlived two husbands. Passages regarding widows are underlined in pencil in her personal Bible. In the margins are written these words that reveal her prayerful distress, "Please help me, O God." What kept her going?

I think of Alice Whiteside McKinnish Smith, and I think of Abraham and Sarah. The outward circumstances of their life do not match their internal state of affairs, but they keep "faithing." Abraham and Sarah's external conditions are not suitable to the promise that God gives them. Sarah has passed the childbearing stage. Their hopes of developing future generations are lost in the Sarah-Hagar-Abraham debacle. Who wants to repeat the complexity of that story? God comes with a promise of children; Abraham and Sarah return the promise with faithfulness, not trusting in the present circumstances but believing in the one who made the promise.

My grandmother told my father and my father told me how Alice would go to the laurel thicket behind their modest mountain home and pray for her children. She prayed for their salvation, for their return home, for their return to God. She saw none of the above. They left her and left her God. Her prayers recorded in the heavens and the storage space of the old trunk, however, reveal that she did not cease believing. Even though she could not see any physical evidence of her prayers, she kept praying. God had promised, and she believed God. She knew that God had said, "I will make you exceedingly fruitful; and I will make nations of you, and kings shall come from you. I will establish my covenant between me and you, and your offspring after you throughout their generations, for an everlasting covenant, to be God to you and to your offspring after you" (Gen. 17:6-7).

Although there was no visible sign of the promise, Alice believed that God would deliver. So she prayed, as evidenced by her words on paper, in letters, in the margins of her Bible, in the laurel thicket while gathering firewood with her small grandchildren. She prayed and trusted God for the future of her family. She died, however, before she was able to see the promise. She was not praying for a fertile womb, for she had given birth to five children. She was not praying for a biological fruitfulness that creates children who in time can create other children. *Fruitful* does not necessarily mean more and more descendants added to the family tree. *Fruitful* can also refer to the kind of life that is full of fruit, a quality rather than quantity of life that adds to the world's rich storehouse of kindness, civility, and praise to the creator God rather than taking away God's goodness from others. Great-grandmother Alice was praying that her children would know God. She even prayed, says my grandmother, that one of her children would become a preacher. The possibility of preacher children was highly unlikely, especially when all her children scorned the church and the gospel. But she prayed.

In 1933 Alice's grandson was born. Alice died five years after his birth, so she never knew that he became a pastor at sixteen years of age, that he would preach almost every Sunday of his life, that his passion would be for people and for God, that he would live his life in the church, weeping for the souls of people as he showed them a better way to live. Alice never knew that her prayers would be answered in her grandson, Harold McKinnish, my father. Likewise, she had no way of knowing that her prayers would extend not only into the next generation but into the next, and the next, and the next. She had no way of predicting that her great-grandchildren would know God and belong to the community of faith, that one day even her great-granddaughter would also become a preacher. God's covenant with Alice, just as with Abraham and Sarah, continues as her faithfulness preserves unknown generations yet to be born.

SUGGESTIONS FOR WORSHIP

Call to Worship
(adapted from Psalm 22:25-26)

LEADER: From you, O God, comes my praise in the great congregation;

PEOPLE: My vows I will pay before those who fear God.

LEADER: The poor shall eat and be satisfied;

PEOPLE: Those who seek God shall praise the Lord.

LEADER: May your hearts live forever! Let us worship God.

Prayer of Confession

God, we confess that we are anxious to know the end from the beginning. We demand to have all the answers sometimes even before the questions are asked. We confess our inability to wait on you and trust your promises for our future. Forgive us for our shortsighted views; our unwillingness to trust; our desire for control; our cavalier attitude toward time. You have promised us that you hold our past, present, and future in your hands. May we rest in your promise that you, O God, know the end from the beginning. Amen.

Assurance of Pardon

LEADER: The God who created time is not bound by time. In response to our confession, this God, working in Christ Jesus, forgives us from our sin. As far as the east is from the west, so far has God removed our sin from us.

PEOPLE: In Christ Jesus we are forgiven.

ALL: Alleluia! Amen.

Benediction

And now may this timeless God give you the courage to face the future, knowing that God knows the end from the beginning and will give us the courage to believe, even when we cannot see. Go in peace. Amen.

Third Sunday in Lent

Linda McKinnish Bridges

Exodus 20:1-17: God's language of covenant is described with ethical obligations in this familiar passage, known as the Decalogue or the Ten Commandments.

Psalm 19: God's laws—similar to the sun that consistently rises and sets and gives warmth and light to all living things— revive the soul, make the simple wise, enlighten the eyes, and are to be desired more than gold.

1 Corinthians 1:18-25: Paul's defense of the gospel is clear, powerful, but full of irony: The cross is a stumbling block to those who will not consider God to be the one hanging from a tree. However, the same cross is a source of power to those who realize that God's strength is best displayed in the human weakness revealed at the crucifixion.

John 2:13-22: In John's Gospel, the story of the Temple cleansing introduces Jesus not only as one who participates with people at a wedding, revealing the power of God with the richness of flowing wine and party conversation (vv. 1-11), but also as one who firmly demands that appropriate ethical conditions be kept in order to sustain a relationship with God.

REFLECTIONS

With striking clarity, these passages call me to consider the "both/and" nature of God. God is not simply a loving God who forsakes standards and ethical norms in order to establish relationships with God's beloved ones. On the other hand, God is not just a demanding deity who requires followers to sign a list of prescribed norms before a relationship can form. God loves freely; Gods demands much.

The tension continues in the words that appear to be polar opposites, *grace* and *law*. The Ten Commandments challenge my postmodern consciousness. As a woman raised in the sixties and taught to challenge standards of absolute authority, I cannot read these words without some soul searching. I reveal my troubling questions to you, which may or may not have troubled the Hebrew children but perhaps may have troubled someone in your listening congregation: Why this long list of prohibitions? Can God's children not be trusted to live the good life? Why did God write out standards? Was it not enough to engage simply in relationship with the people and assume that the right standards would evolve from a healthy relationship?

What do the Ten Commandments really mean? I know the textbook answer: that they are God's guidelines for God's people, to ensure health, well-being, and a high quality of life. But are these prerequisite to a relationship with Yahweh God? Could the people have thought, "If I follow these rules, will God love me?" If they did not think it then, the New Testament reminds us that they thought of it later, so much that Paul had to preach "justification by faith" over and over again.

The New Testament lesson, the story of the cleansing of the Temple, offers no immediate consolation. Jesus, who loves sinners and unclean people, goes through the Temple, upsetting tables and demanding that the merchants clean up their acts immediately. The task of this preaching assignment is to move beyond the easy answers of this passage and set the demands of God in the context of a postmodern culture grown tired of absolutes and meaningless prohibitions. God wants people to live right, but how and why?

A SERMON BRIEF

Mack was our firstborn dog. We had Mack before we had Kyle, our son. We found Mack in the local animal shelter, sick and isolated from the rest of the puppies. We were told he had been mistreated. For some reason he was the one we wanted. We chose the sick little furry white terrier to be one of our family. And Mack was just that, as only animal lovers can understand.

The beautiful, passive ball of puppy fur turned into a canine mound of boundless, bubbly energy. As he grew into an adult dog, although he remained short and stocky, he jumped fences, raced every dog in the neighborhood, and delighted in the freedom of life. He was beautiful to watch as he delighted in jumping in the air as high as he could, whether to retrieve a biscuit, snap at an innocent bird, or escape from our carefully fenced yard. No obstacle was too high, no place was too confined, no dog too large for dear Mack.

Mack's spirit of unlimited freedom hurt him on occasion. One time, he jumped out of the fenced yard to chase a car and almost lost his life in the process. We found him in the road barely breathing. We took him home to check his injuries. The next morning when we prepared to go to the vet, he had perked up and was fine. Another time, he was involved in a car accident and ran away to die. We searched the neighborhood on foot and by car and alerted the neighbors that Mack had disappeared. We could not find him. In a few days we discovered Mack under the cool of the car, sleeping. His fur was matted with blood and his eyes looked tired, but he was alive. Mack survived his reckless quest for freedom. He continued to move with great speed, jumping over whatever obstacle with sheer delight.

We moved to a new home in a busy suburb filled with children and lots of cars, Mack's favorite things. We immediately fenced the backyard for Mack. We placed the doghouse in the center of the wooded area. There was shade and sun and lots of space for dear Mack to run. Surely, he could be content here, we thought. The fence posts were high enough, or so we surmised, to keep Mack from making even his best jump. The wood measured over five feet high and Mack was less than two feet tall; we thought we had our Mack confined.

Then came the day when he took a running leap and cleared the tall fence posts by at least two feet. This dog could fly! And so it was that one night Mack "flew" out of the fence, sprinted into the road in the darkness, and was hit by a car. But once again, this dog with the multiple lives of a cat bounced back—after a trip to the vet and some good nursing by his human custodians.

But these human custodians were becoming weary. And we were torn. We loved to watch Mack's elaborate displays of freedom. We delighted with him as he soared in the air, celebrating his Napoleonic frame that could squirm, turn, catch a ball or bone, all while still high in the air. We loved to watch him. Watching him made us feel alive and happy. But we also wanted our little dog to stay alive.

So we established even tighter boundaries that we knew would preserve his life. We built taller fences, tried to tame him through obedience training, made him wear a leash. In the evenings we chained him to a stake, close to his doghouse, confining him to the yard, yet giving him space to move around. We gave him freedom when we could, but within the boundaries that we knew would spare his life. The choices were simple: be free and die or be confined and live.

Unfortunately, Mack chose the former option. One morning my husband went out to feed Mack, release his chain, and give him freedom to run freely in the backyard. What he found, however, would stay in our minds for years. He discovered that our precious dog Mack had loved freedom so much that he had once again tried to "fly" over the fence, unaware that a chain circled his neck. Once he cleared the fence, the chain was too short to let Mack reach the ground. And our dear Mack dangled from the chain and died during the night without a sound.

We, of course, were devastated. We were sad that our little ball of fur and canine delight was gone. We saw in graphic detail what happens when one chooses life without any boundaries. Mack hated fences or any kind of border that inhibited his movement. He deplored prohibitions. In his campaign against boundaries, however, he died a senseless death. His love for unbounded freedom killed him. If Mack could have learned to live with even a limited amount of restrictions, he would be at our feet today. But he chose to defy our every attempt to make him safe, comfortable within established space. And in that defiance, he chose death.

Could it be this simple? Could God have known that it was not enough simply to say, "Be holy, children of Israel." Those boundaries of ethical living called the Ten Commandments are intended to give life, not take it away. To commit adultery kills relationships and covenants made between people in communities. To steal destroys a sense of sharing and trust. Wanting something that does not belong to you kills a part of your own sense of self and confidence. Murder destroys that which God has created. Bearing false witness prevents honest relationships between people. Idolatry kills our image of God who cannot be contained in any one single image. Not resting on the sabbath violates a harmony of life that combines spiritual and physical refreshment with the demands of work. Honorable family relationships create family trees of ethical stability for future generations to follow.

The boundaries are designed not to limit us but to set us free in ways that limit our own self-destruction. The Ten Commandments are not absolutes given from an angry God who likes to see us squirm as we desperately try to keep the rules. The Ten Commandments are commonsense boundary markers that promise a life worth living for oneself and others.

It seems simple. Keep the rules and everyone will live lives worth living. Just post these boundary markers on the walls of courtrooms, classrooms, and Sunday school rooms and our society will live happily thereafter. Yet you and I know that it does not work this way. In those courtrooms where the Ten Commandments are placed, people are still breaking the law. In classrooms, schoolchildren sometimes steal pencils, cheat on tests, and even kill one another. In Sunday school rooms, where the rules have been posted for years, people are still worshiping the gods of consumerism and military strength. Simply to post the rules, either etched in stone or framed with glass, is not enough.

In our Gospel reading for today, Jesus cleansed the Temple. And in so doing, he was establishing boundaries, of course. The place of worship had been violated. Religious laws had been ignored. The Commandments had been forgotten. Jesus' actions of anger gave a pointed lesson to those in the Temple that day.

But it is not enough just to mark the boundaries; one must also give of oneself. Jesus' life was taken as an example of what happens when the boundaries are unmarked. From one perspective, the story is one of a senseless death that could have been eliminated if people had been more attentive to religious respect and open to one another. But death was not averted. And Jesus' life and death remind us that in the marking of boundaries for ourselves and others, we are to provide not only the rules for life, but also the love that shows us how to live between the boundary lines.

The law comes packaged with limits, with boundaries. Grace comes undeserved, unlimited. In the life and death of Christ, the lines of law and grace converge and we see God. Choose life with boundaries and live. Choose life without boundaries and die. And the living God will provide relationships with others and with Christ that will make those markers clear and will offer a life worth living.

SUGGESTIONS FOR WORSHIP

Call to Worship (adapted from Psalm 19:7-9)

LEADER: The law of the Lord is perfect;
PEOPLE: It revives the soul.

LEADER: The decrees of the Lord are sure;
PEOPLE: They make wise the simple.
LEADER: The precepts of the Lord are right;
PEOPLE: The heart rejoices.
LEADER: The commandment of the Lord is clear.
PEOPLE: The eyes are enlightened.
ALL: Let us worship God.

Prayer of Confession

God of law and grace, mercy and justice, you continue to amaze us. We try to place you and your work within our own frames of thought, and we are always surprised. We work hard to keep your law, then we learn that you love us even if we miss the mark. We let go of the boundaries of ethical norms, then we learn that you make demands and requirements on our life. We cannot fully understand the infinite mind of an infinite God who loves and demands, who gives and requires, who provides grace and law.

Teach us your ways so that our lives might be preserved. Protect us from ourselves. Keep us from destruction. May your commandments be the guideposts to fuller living—not death. And then, O gracing God, when we do stumble, when we do fail to keep your law, forgive us with your tender mercies. Help us start again. For you, O God, and only you, are able to hold both the power of grace and the strength of the law in your hands. May we learn your ways, O God. In the name of the one who cleansed the Temple and then gave his life as a living sacrifice, Jesus Christ, we pray. Amen.

Benediction

Now go with the peace that comes from knowing that God's perfect love is matched by God's perfect law. Go in this God, who both loves us and demands that we find life—in this world and in the world to come. Amen.

Fourth Sunday in Lent

Alyce M. McKenzie

Numbers 21:4-9: The book of Numbers gets its name from the two "numberings" it includes of "the whole congregation" of Israel (chaps. 1, 26). Each census is limited to adult males of military age, which speaks volumes about the value the community placed on women and children. The Hebrew name for the book means "in the wilderness."

This passage reveals the original Exodus generation following their pattern of remembering their own grievances and forgetting God's past faithfulness. The same God loosens the consequences of sin on the people and provides their antidote. The serpent serves as a double metaphor. It represents those exercises of memory that lead to death in struggling communities. It also represents those that lead to life. This text reflects memories of a bronze serpent (Neshutan) mentioned as being present in Solomon's Temple (2 Kings 18:4; Wisd. of Sol. 16:1-7).

Psalm 107:1-3, 17-22: This hymn of national thanksgiving for God's faithfulness in the wilderness is an exercise in faithful remembering. It includes a priestly summons to various groups to testify to their memories and present experiences of God's saving grace (vv. 4-32).

Ephesians 2:1-10: The book of Ephesians is a theological reminder to churches in Asia Minor of their unity in Christ. God mercifully provides the antidote to the death we endure because of our disobedience and disunity and raises us up to new life in Jesus Christ. One in him, we grow into a faithful community, a beacon of light to the world. Our life-giving function is analogous to that fulfilled by the serpent in the wilderness.

. . .

. . .

John 3:14-21: This text discerns an analogy between two life-giving agents: the serpent in the wilderness and the Son. Having descended from heaven, now, like the serpent, the Son of Man has been lifted up, and is the antidote to death through disobedience.

REFLECTIONS

This Lent in our spiritual pilgrimage we have accompanied Jesus in his ministry through times of great joy and deep pathos. In the days ahead he faces his greatest obstacles yet. The quality of our discipleship will depend on how we use our memories. Will we press ahead with him, energized by the active memory of God's faithfulness, as the psalmist urges us to do? Or will we be mindful only of fears within and obstacles without? We need a lesson in the faithful exercise of memory to prepare us for what lies ahead.

A SERMON BRIEF

Remember to Forget; Forget to Remember

"We Jews are a community based on memory," says theologian Martin Buber. Says feminist Jewish scholar Judith Plaskow, "It is in telling the story of the past as Jews that we learn who we truly are in the present" (Judith Plaskow, *Standing Again at Sinai: Judaism from a Feminist Perspective* [San Francisco: HarperSanFrancisco, 1990], 29).

For communities of Christians as well as for our Jewish brothers and sisters, the matter of memory is crucial. "What will we remember?" is a good question to guide us during this Lenten season of self-examination. It determines whether we press on in faith or fall back into bondage. The book of Numbers as a whole, and especially this slithering serpent story, is an attempt to answer the question, What kinds of remembering and forgetting lead to death for communities, and which ones lead to life?

Since setting out from the wilderness of Sinai the Israelites have followed a recurring pattern of remembering their misfortunes and forgetting God's faithfulness. Now in the twenty-first chapter of

Numbers, irritated because the King of Edom won't let them cut through his yard to get to the Promised Land, they once again focus on their impatience and irritation and voice it in complaints. This time there's no time for Moses to kneel and intercede for them with God. It's as if God serves them up a mini-plague to help them remember the way it really was in Egypt!

We twentieth century wanderers can't deny the glaring similarities between the Israelites' faulty memory syndrome and our own.

Do you know anyone who remembers a past that never was? This is the "Egypt wasn't so bad" syndrome. "We had all-you-can-eat smorgasbords every night, didn't we?" (Num. 11:5, paraphrase). "Why have you brought us up out of Egypt to die in the wilderness?" (Num. 21:5). A church tells its new pastor, "In the sixties we had twice as many members! People these days just don't come to church like they used to." A woman who has left her abusive spouse voices her second thoughts. "Maybe I shouldn't have left him. He could be so loving at times." Another family member tells a woman having flashbacks to episodes of childhood sexual abuse, "Why don't you just move on with your life and stop rehashing these unhealthy memories? They probably never happened." We numb ourselves with nostalgia as a way of avoiding the challenge of the present.

Do you know anybody who forgets what they should remember? Sometimes we forget our own leadership responsibilities and place all blame for setbacks and all our great expectations on the leader's shoulders. Church members turn to the paid staff and the core of active membership and say, "Show us the attendance increases. Show us the programs. Show us the money." A thirtysomething professional with two young children said to her pastor recently, "My life in every other category is so stressed that when it comes to church, I'm in a receiving mode."

I have been involved in a clergywomen's group since the 1980s. We spent the first half of the decade sharing memories of discrimination that ought not be forgotten, decrying the statistics pointing to inequitable representation of women in leadership roles and differences in salary between men and women. This was and continues to be important work to do. But somewhere in the middle of the decade our focus shifted. We began to celebrate the work accomplished by the Miriams of past decades and to combine our efforts to gain access to leadership positions in various boards and agencies, working with our male colleagues to build the future God was calling us to claim.

Without forgetting what we needed to remember, we began to remember God's promise to lead us forward.

Do you know any communities who forget the contributions of traditionally silenced groups within society? Someone once said of theologian and social activist Simone Weil, who starved herself to death to maintain solidarity with French workers in wartime, that she was "herself erased," but with the erasure underlined (Iris Rozencwajg, "Take Care, Then, How You Listen: My Spiritual Mothers," *Daughters of Sarah* [Winter 1995]).

This description fits the depiction of women in the book of Numbers. Women are absent from its censuses and, with the exception of Miriam, from public religious leadership. Women are viewed as possessions of males (Num. 14:3; 30:1-16), and as posing troublesome exceptions to male rules (chaps. 27, 36). Women and children suffer invisibly throughout the narrative from the policies of those in power.

Judith Plaskow writes, "Women's voices and experiences have been largely invisible in the record of Jewish belief and experience that has come down to us. . . . Confronting this silence raises disturbing questions. . . . What would have been different had the great silence been filled?" (Judith Plaskow, *Standing Again at Sinai: Judaism from a Feminist Perspective* [San Francisco: HarperSanFrancisco, 1990], 1). Many groups within our society and churches have been made invisible by the faulty memory of dominant interests. This question, "What would have been different had the great silence been filled?" cries out to be asked and answered in our own Christian traditions. Its answer is that time will tell, as women, men, youth, and children look to our life-giving savior, whose presence is the antidote that can heal our faulty memories. Remembering to look to Christ, we shed his life-giving light on all the shadow-shrouded places. We become what God created us to be: faith communities of forward-looking courage, accountability, and respectful diversity.

"This little light of mine, I'm gonna let it shine." This African American spiritual was the signature song of civil rights leader Fannie Lou Hamer. The youngest of twenty children, Fannie was born in 1917 to a destitute Mississippi sharecropping family. Her parents taught her about a God who helps us endure sufferings as well as empowers us to lift ourselves out of them. Fannie's mother embodied this strength, at one point standing up to a white overseer who slapped one of her sons, an act for which she might have been killed.

While Fannie yearned for learning, she was put to work chopping cotton. Though she and her husband yearned for children of their own, she was sterilized without her consent by a white doctor. Though she loved and practiced peace, her involvement in the voting rights campaign for Blacks got her arrested, fired, and severely beaten. A national and international civil rights leader, she ran for Congress, campaigned against the Vietnam War, for Head Start, and for employment rights for single mothers.

Fannie thought of her life, not as one remembered grievance after another, but as one divine victory after another. Near death in 1977, she told friends, family, and colleagues to remember that "no one is free until we are all free." Fannie's signature song, the soundtrack of her life, was the gospel song, "This little light of mine, I'm going to let it shine." Fannie would have added "and everyone else's too!" (Mary Krane Derr, "Women in Ministry: Letting Everyone's Light Shine: The Life and Work of Fannie Lou Hamer (1917–1977)," *Daughters of Sarah* [Fall 1994]: 20-22).

In between Sinai and the Promised Land is where we all live this Lent, and it's not an easy place to be. By God's grace, as we continue our journey together, let us not for one moment forget to remember God's presence, God's provision, and God's promise, even Jesus Christ our Lord!

SUGGESTIONS FOR WORSHIP

Call to Worship

LEADER: Oh give thanks to the Lord who is merciful and just.

PEOPLE: God's steadfast love endures forever!

LEADER: As the redeemed of the Lord, bring offerings of praise to the holy one.

PEOPLE: We were wanderers, and God corrected and directed us.
We were in prison, and God cut in two the bars of iron.
We were sick unto death, and God saved us from our distress.

ALL: Thanks be to the Lord who is merciful and just!

Prayer of Confession

Just and gracious God, we confess that we have forgotten what we should have remembered and been preoccupied with things better left forgotten. We have not appreciated the gift of your sustaining presence. At the smallest of obstacles, our faith has balked. We have become irritable and impatient, ready to give up. In the face of the deepest sufferings of those around us, we have been quite willing to avert our gazes and our thoughts. Forgive us for the hotness of our tempers and the coldness of our hearts. Strengthen us as we face the consequences of our past actions. Into your just and loving hands we place this present moment. Into an uncertain future we walk, certain of your presence, your provision, and your promise.

Assurance of Pardon

Our God is merciful and gracious, slow to anger, abounding in steadfast love and faithfulness, keeping steadfast love for the thousandth generation, forgiving iniquity and transgression and sin. I declare to you in the name of Jesus Christ, you are forgiven. Amen.

Benediction

Go forth in boldness, willing to risk words and deeds of justice, strengthened by the justice of God.

Go forth in peace, knowing that you are forgiven.

Go forth in joy, knowing that you have been raised to new and eternal life in Jesus Christ.

Fifth Sunday in Lent

Leonora Tubbs Tisdale

Jeremiah 31:31-34: "I will write [my covenant] on their hearts."

Psalm 51:1-12: "Create in me a clean heart, O God."

Hebrews 5:5-10: Christ is appointed high priest by God.

John 12:20-33: Those who love Christ must follow in the way of service.

REFLECTIONS

When preaching I am often drawn to symbols that emerge either from the biblical text, from contemporary life, or from the two in dialogue. In this instance, it was the juxtaposition of the Jeremiah text (focusing upon the new covenant God will write upon our hearts) with the Valentine's Day poem written by my son when he was in elementary school ("When It Rained Hearts") that provided me with imagery through which I could witness to both the wonder and the mystery of God's great gift of the heart to us on Golgotha. Liturgically, I was also very aware that the visible symbols of that costly new covenant of God's love—bread and wine—would be spread before my congregation on the table as I preached.

A SERMON BRIEF

When It Rained Hearts

I am one of those people who likes to hold on to a season or a holiday as long as possible. So it is usually only about this time of year that I finally get around to taking the red and white Valentine's Day cards out of my kitchen window and relegating them to my box of personal keepsakes. Sometimes, in the process of storing this year's cards away for posterity, I browse through the cards of the past, and nearly always they make me smile.

In my box, for instance, there is a valentine given me by my sixteen-year-old son when he was a first grader. What makes me chuckle as I read it is not only the corny joke that adorns its pages, but also my memory of the way in which my son presented it to me: doubled over with unsuppressed laughter and repeatedly asking, "Mom, do you get it? Do you get it?" Resting in my box is also a Valentine given to me by my daughter—now a college freshman—when she was a preteen. The confiding tone of that card reminds me of how precious those years were while she was living at home, and of how much I miss her now that she's gone. And, of course, there are plenty of sweet, sentimental cards from my beloved husband—a man who knows his spouse well enough after all these years to also know that I never, ever get tired of his professions of undying devotion. Covered with hearts, most of them are, and, for this mom and wife, symbolic of all that is best and noblest and truest in the human heart.

But I am also aware enough of the rest of the world to know that for many, perhaps for some of you, Valentine's Day does not symbolize all that is best and noblest and truest in the human heart. I overheard a group of single people talking among themselves last Cupid's day, and one of them said that for her—with no "significant other"—it was one of the most difficult holidays of the year. I know it was a tough day for a friend, who has recently been through a painful divorce. Certainly it was difficult, as well, for all those folk who stood a long, long time in front of the Hallmark displays, knowing they were supposed to give a card, but having a hard time finding a card that didn't lie about the true nature of the relationship in which they're bound.

Even on Valentine's Day—especially on Valentine's Day—we are reminded not only of what is best and noblest and truest about the human heart; we are also reminded of what is lonely and painful and faithless about the human heart. Despite the cheery greeting card illusion, we still live in a world where hurtful words and deeds pierce the human heart, where fragile hearts are crushed by broken relationships, and where Sergeant Pepper's Lonely Hearts Club Band could find a ready audience. Somehow, despite all our inner longing for deep and lasting and loving relationships, we humans still hurt one another—even in the midst of our deepest professions of love.

In that regard, not much has changed about human nature since the seventh century B.C. when the prophet Jeremiah spoke the words we read this morning. Israel, according to Jeremiah, had a heart problem. And it not only affected their relationships with one another, it also affected their relationship with their God.

Israel, who had been wed to God through the covenant at Sinai, had broken God's heart. Like a faithless spouse, Israel had lusted—or, to use Jeremiah's more graphic language, gone whoring—after other gods. Like a lying spouse, Israel had said, "Yes, yes," to keeping God's commands chiseled on those Sinai tables, but had yielded to the temptation to break those vows time and time again. Indeed, so adept had God's people become at doing evil that the prophet says of them, "My people are foolish, they do not know me; they are stupid children, they have no understanding. They are skilled in doing evil, but do not know how to do good" (Jer. 4:22).

This total corruption, of course, had also affected Israel's relationships with other people. Despite God's command that the covenant people treat the widows, orphans, and needy ones in their midst with justice, they failed to do so. Although they went about their daily routines with a facade of red and white cheerfulness, underneath lay a corruption of the heart so deep and so intense that this prophet sees no cure, save for a transplant.

And so God announces through the prophet, "This is the covenant that I will make with the house of Israel . . . : I will put my law within them, and I will write it on their hearts; and I will be their God, and they shall be my people" (Jer. 31:33). God will remove the heart grown hard like the stone on which the broken commandments were etched, and replace it with a new heart, sealed with a new covenant, with the law of God written not without, but within.

It is easy for some of us to suppose those words of drastic measures are intended for others less faithful than we. Yet I dare say that if we would allow the words of the prophet to cut through the illusions through which we like to view our own hearts—if we would see our hearts as they truly are—we would find that we, too, are in need of a transplant.

Who among us has not seen pain etched on the faces of loved ones that we've hurt through our betrayal or venomous words or sheer thoughtlessness? Who among us has not known captivity to bad and harmful habits—when the good that we would do we seem unable to do, and the evil we do not want to do has us in its vice grip? Who among us has not watched our noblest intentions to give our lives, or even a significant portion thereof, to helping the hungry or poor or homeless, become buried under other priorities? And who among us has not experienced great difficulty in treating the least of these with the same respect we would give to Christ?

Like the Israelites, we know the gnawing emptiness that comes from prostituting ourselves for other gods. Thus, the horror of this passage from Jeremiah is that these same, stark, judging, angry words could also be addressed to us. For at times, we, like Israel, "are skilled in doing evil, but do not know how to do good."

But if the judgment is ours, the promise is ours, too—a promise that this season of Lent and this Communion table of Christ's passion remind us has already begun to be fulfilled in our midst. For our Lord Jesus, on the very night he was betrayed, *betrayed* by a dear friend, took the cup and said, "This cup is the new covenant, sealed in my blood. Do this as often as you drink it in remembrance of me."

And when on the next day he was crucified and the shattering of the very heart of God echoed throughout all creation, a new covenant was sealed. And God, our compassionate and merciful and ever-faithful spouse, found us when we could not find ourselves, and brought us back into relationship with our beloved.

Theologian Karl Barth has a wonderful sermon on this passage from Jeremiah, and in language reminiscent of the children's game, "Mother, May I?" it is simply titled "You May" (Karl Barth, "You May," in *Call for God*, trans. A. T. Mackay [New York: Harper & Row, 1967], 19-27). The miracle of this new covenant sealed in Christ's blood, and of the new heart given us through the covenant, says Barth, is that all those terrifying "thou shalts" that once stood outside us—"Thou shalt have no other gods before me; thou shalt not make any graven image; thou shalt not lie or steal or commit adultery or covet"—have now been consumed under the gracious "you may" of God. The good that we were unable to do ourselves, God in Christ has given us the freedom, the liberty to do.

And what is the command of this new covenant that God will write upon our hearts? It is simply this: that we let God love us. That we allow ourselves to be totally bowled over by a God who expressed love for us faithless adulterers through the outpouring of God's all for us on Golgotha. For you see, it is only as we open ourselves to receive the depths and heights of love this amazing and this divine that we are given a new heart—a heart that is freed to love God with its entirety and to love our neighbors as we love ourselves.

My son William—the one who likes to give funny valentines—was in his elementary years an aspiring poet. One of the treasures of my keepsake box is a valentine William made for me when he was seven years old, a valentine covered with hearts and containing a fanciful poem William himself had written. The poem, entitled "When It Rained Hearts," recounts a number of strange and wonderful things that happened on a day when hearts fell from the heavens like rain: cows and horses finding themselves on the wrong side of the fence; mom jumping out of bed and dying her hair; yellow jackets swarming the trees, a little boy having to wear his raincoat to school, and a dog who thinks all this is mighty cool.

But it's the last verse of the poem I particularly want to share with you. The last verse goes like this:

> And how it rained hearts, nobody knows.
> Still, it's a mystery, I suppose.

The good news of this Lenten season and of this table spread before us is that a long time ago on God's Valentine's Day, it rained hearts. The Lord whom we had betrayed refused to betray us, and instead poured out his own heart for us that we might receive new hearts. The law, once written without, was sealed upon our hearts by his own blood. And the terrifying "thou shalts" of the first covenant became the gracious "you mays" of the new.

And how it rained hearts, nobody knows. When all's said and done, it's still a marvelous mystery, don't you suppose?

SUGGESTIONS FOR WORSHIP

Call to Worship

LEADER: We come, seeking Jesus, who is for us the way, the truth, the life.

PEOPLE: We come, seeking Jesus, whose way leads to the cross, whose truth leads to suffering love, and whose life was poured out for us all.

LEADER: We come, seeking Jesus, who calls us to follow in this way, this truth, and this life.

PEOPLE: We come, seeking Jesus, whose love alone can empower us so to do.

Prayer of Confession (Psalm 51:1-3, 10-12)

(In unison.) Have mercy on me, O God, according to your steadfast love; according to your abundant mercy blot out my transgressions. Wash me thoroughly from my iniquity, and cleanse me from my sin. For I know my transgressions, and my sin is ever before me. Create in me a clean heart, O God, and put a new and right spirit within me. Do not cast me away from your presence, and do not take your holy spirit from me. Restore to me the joy of your salvation, and sustain in me a willing spirit. (A period of silence follows.)

Assurance of Pardon
(adapted from Jeremiah 31:31-34)

LEADER: The days are surely coming, says the Lord, when I will make a new covenant with my people. I will put my law within them, and I will write it on their hearts. I will be their God, and they shall be my people. For I will forgive their iniquity, and remember their sin no more.

Friends, believe the good news. In Jesus Christ the new covenant of God has been sealed upon our hearts. Our sins are forgiven, and we are set free to love others as God in Christ has first loved us.

PEOPLE: **Thanks be to God!**

Benediction

With hearts made new, let us go forth to love the Lord our God with all our heart, soul, mind, and strength, and our neighbors as ourselves. The grace of our Lord Jesus Christ be with you all.

Passion/Palm Sunday

Eunjoo Mary Kim

Liturgy of the Passion

Isaiah 50:4-9a: "I gave my back to those who struck me, and my cheeks to those who pulled out the beard; I did not hide my face from insult and spitting."

Psalm 31:9-16: "Be gracious to me, O LORD, for I am in distress; my eye wastes away from grief, my soul and body also."

Philippians 2:5-11: "Let the same mind be in you that was in Christ Jesus, who, though he was in the form of God, did not regard equality with God as something to be exploited, but emptied himself, taking the form of a slave, being born in human likeness."

Mark 14:1–15:47: "While [Jesus] was at Bethany in the house of Simon the leper, as he sat at the table, a woman came with an alabaster jar of very costly ointment of nard, and she broke open the jar and poured the ointment on his head."

REFLECTIONS

During Holy Week, which begins with Palm Sunday or Passion Sunday, we commemorate God's redeeming work through Jesus' suffering, death on the cross, and resurrection. The passion narrative in the Gospel of Mark, which begins in chapter 14, tells us of the suffering of Jesus Christ. It starts with the story of Jesus' visit to the house of Simon the leper in Bethany just a few days after his triumphal entrance into Jerusalem. The act of an unnamed woman, who poured costly perfume on Jesus' head, reminded those who followed Jesus that he had already foretold his death. Just as God's salvation has been fulfilled through Jesus' suffering, so the disciple is to follow Jesus in the way of cross, imitating Christ's humility.

A SERMON BRIEF

When the disciples gathered around Jesus at the house of Simon the leper, the mood must have been one of excitement. Only a few days before they had seen Jesus process into Jerusalem in a kingly manner—surely one of their greatest experiences since they first began following him. Although Jesus had marched into the holy city on a path covered not by a red carpet but by the leaves of trees, riding not on a fine horse but on a little colt, and sitting not on a golden saddle but on someone's garments stinking with sweat, this parade, for the disciples, had still been far better than any other king's procession. For as Jesus entered Jerusalem, throngs of people who had known his miraculous power followed Jesus and shouted with joy, "Hosanna, the king of the Jews! Blessed is the one who comes in the name of the Lord!" And do you know what? The disciples were there amidst all the uproar, walking right behind Jesus with pride and dignity.

Now, several days later, Jesus and the disciples have gathered at the home of a leper. While some may wonder why he chose a leper's house for dinner, it's really not surprising when we remember that Jesus' best friends were outcasts: the blind, the mute, the demon-possessed, and tax collectors. Indeed, Jesus was the hero of such marginalized people. He healed their diseases, liberated them from their sins, and restored their relationships with God and other people. It was no wonder then, that people such as these followed Jesus and supported him as the king of Jews. They had great hopes and expectations that Jesus would one day overturn the unjust political structures of their day and establish a new kingdom in which the upper classes no longer exploited the underclass, but instead shared their benefits with them.

Although the crowd and Jesus' disciples believed that the new kingdom might be established by Jesus' miraculous power, Jesus, on the other hand, had repeatedly told his disciples that he would suffer and die on a cross and then immediately rise from the dead. But somehow they never understood his words. In fact, they *did not want* to understand.

Do you remember when Jesus foretold his death and resurrection in Caesarea Philippi? Peter was very distressed and took him aside and rebuked him, "Teacher, please don't say these things. See this huge crowd following you. No one wants you to die like that. We don't understand resurrection. Please don't confuse us with such silly words."

When the disciples were on the way to Jerusalem, Jesus again talked about his death and resurrection. But no one paid attention to it. Instead, James and his brother John came forward and said, "Teacher, when you become the king of Israel, please let us sit at your right and left hands in your glory."

Once, twice, three times . . . Jesus yet again reminded them that the salvation of God would be fulfilled by his suffering and death on the cross and his exaltation from death. However, they could not understand what he was saying because of their vested interests and prejudiced minds.

Because they had consistently ignored or misunderstood Jesus' own teachings about his suffering and death, I rather imagine that the disciples in the house of Simon the leper were still in an excited mood as they talked about the blueprint for a new kingdom. As long as Jesus was with them, working miracles as he had done before—like feeding five thousand people with two fish and five loaves of bread—they could even think that their revolutionary kingdom would be prosperous.

Jesus, on the other hand, knew that his time was near an end. His terrifying death was coming closer every second. One of his beloved disciples would soon betray him, handing him over to the chief priests and the scribes. The religious authorities would condemn him, spit on him, flog him, and kill him on a cross. The crowd who now followed him because of his miraculous power would soon scatter, hiding like scared cats, disheartened by his death. Even God, his father, would be silent in this time of suffering in order to give him the name that was above every name.

Who would know this mind of Jesus?

At that moment, something very strange happened in the house of the leper. A woman entered the room where Jesus and his disciples were sitting. She entered a place reserved for men only.

Some of you may know about the Jewish patriarchal culture of that time. The second-century Jewish rabbi Judah ben Elai represented early Jewish society very well when he said that Jewish men should thank God every day for three things: first, not being born a Gentile; second, not being born a *woman*; and third, not being illiterate, so that they could study the Torah. I am sure this sexist culture found no exception in the house of Simon. The room prepared for Jesus was for men only.

But in the middle of their conversation, a woman entered boldly and unabashedly, holding an alabaster jar. Disregarding the disciples' embarrassment over her interruption, she then broke the jar and poured the costly ointment on Jesus' head. And suddenly, the room that had been filled with the odor of sweat and the steam of men's breath was refreshed by the sweet scent of this perfume.

Recovering from their surprise, some of the disciples grumbled to one another, "Why was the ointment wasted in this way?" "Woman, don't you know how costly it is? It's worth three hundred denarii—one year's salary for a laborer! If you had given that to us, we could have sold it and given the money to the poor. What a foolish and impulsive thing you did!"

Jesus' response to her and to them, however, was quite different, and quite amazing: "She has done what she could," he said of the woman. "She has anointed my body before its burial. She has prepared me for my death."

In Jewish custom, the dead body was anointed with fragrant spices before burial. But Jesus' body would have no opportunity for anointing before his burial. The woman's symbolic action, then, prepared Jesus for his death.

Who was this woman? We don't know. What was her name? We don't know that either. Unlike Mary Magdalene, Mary the mother of James, or Salome, who are named in the Bible, this woman is not identified by name—even though Jesus said of her, "Wherever the good news is proclaimed in the whole world, what she has done will be told in remembrance of her" (Mark 14:9). We don't even know the names of her husband or her son.

What we do know is that this unnamed woman showed her love for Jesus in the right way. And the fragrance that filled the room was enough to remind the disciples of Jesus' previous predictions of his death. The kingdom of God, this act reminded them, does not come by miraculous works of power. Rather, it comes through the self-sacrificing love of God. Jesus' kingly procession led to humiliation and to death, even death on a cross. Yet it was through such obedience that Jesus became king of kings, the promised messiah. This is the way of God's salvation.

Today, we have gathered together around Jesus in the house of God, just as his disciples gathered around him in Simon's house. We have many things to do during this gathering: discuss politics and economics, talk about our children's education and church policies, plan mission projects and fellowship events, and so forth. But what we really need is the fragrance that reminds us of the suffering and death of Christ.

Do we have the mind of Jesus? Is our church filled with the heat of human enthusiasm or with the fragrance of the suffering servant, our Jesus Christ?

The way of discipleship is the way of Golgotha, imitating Christ's humility.

SUGGESTIONS FOR WORSHIP

Call to Worship
(adapted from Isaiah 50 and Psalm 31)

LEADER: The Lord God helps us.
PEOPLE: And we know that we shall not be put to shame.
LEADER: It is the Lord God who helps us.
PEOPLE: Who will declare us guilty?
LEADER: We trust in you, O Lord.
PEOPLE: We say, "You are our God!"
LEADER: Let your face shine upon your servants.
PEOPLE: Save us in your steadfast love!

Prayer of Confession

Although we say by the tongue that we are your disciples called by grace, our lives have not shown your truth to the world, O God. We desire our own names to be glorified, rather than exalting your name through our obedience to the point of death. We trust our limited knowledge and experience, rather than following your way of salvation through suffering and humility. God of mercy, forgive our sins and renew our spirits with the fragrance of your sacrificial death on the cross. Amen.

Assurance of Pardon

LEADER: My dear sisters and brothers, your sins are forgiven by the flogging, mocking, and crucifying of Jesus Christ, who is the Lord of lords and the King of kings.
PEOPLE: Thanks be to God!

Benediction

May the fragrance of God's sacrificial love fill this congregation. And may we follow Jesus with obedience and humility, in remembrance of her, who prepared for the death of our Lord. Amen.

Holy Thursday

Adele Stiles Resmer

Exodus 12:1-4 (5-10), 11-14: God instructs Moses and Aaron to prepare a festival meal that will remind the Israelites of God's passing over them so they might be delivered from Egypt.

Psalm 116:1-2, 12-19: The psalm begins with professions of love for God who has responded to the calls of one in need. Because God has responded, the psalmist continues with promises of fulfilling vows, servanthood, and thanksgiving sacrifice.

1 Corinthians 11:23-26: Using what have become for us the "words of institution," Paul passes on the proper observance of the Lord's Supper to the Corinthian church.

John 13:1-17, 31b-35: Jesus takes on the role of a servant by washing the feet of the disciples, thus providing the example for his command to "love one another as I have loved you."

REFLECTIONS

The traditional Holy Thursday text is rich with possibilities: foot washing as an example of servanthood; servanthood as the inbreaking of the kingdom of God; the commandment to love one another. As familiar as this text is to me, when I read it again, there is more here than I can take in. After reading the text through several times (with and without the verses omitted by the lectionary of Jesus' encounter with Judas), I wait to see what images emerge. My mind keeps returning to a Jesus bending down, lifting the feet of his disciples, washing their feet. So this image and its contrast become the defining elements of the sermon.

A SERMON BRIEF

These days our eyes and ears are regularly drawn to the big, the spectacular, the loud, and the jarring. We flock to movies with special effects that loom larger than life. A ship cracks in half before our eyes, walls of water rush toward us, almost as if to surge off the screen. A huge monster stomps across the screen and we hear and practically feel the earth move beneath our seats. Machine gun blasts light up before our eyes and fill our ears with the horrific sounds of people shrieking and wailing in ear-splitting decibels. A recent survey shows that the volume of popular movies has increased to the level of jets taking off, matching the larger-than-life events taking place on the screen.

It is true that there are gentle movies with subtle, delicate movements, but the numbers of us who go to such films pale in comparison with those who frequent the spectacular, the extravagant, the broad-sweeping. We seem drawn to the sensory extravaganza, the eye-popping, ear-splitting, earth-shaking events played out before us on the screen. When friends and I discuss these films, the key word that emerges repeatedly is "escape." Escape from everyday pressures, escape from responsibilities, escape from the boring, the disappointing, the mundane (even if for only a couple of hours).

While a little break every now and then is not all bad, the expectation of "WOW" at each seating inadvertently dulls our senses to the simple, the quiet, the ambling, both on the screen and in life. Our conditioning in the larger-than-life makes it difficult to see or hear or be interested in something just life-sized. How much easier it would be if our partners and children were bigger and better than life; in their ordinariness, we often don't see who they are. How much more exciting if our work changed the future of humankind; the mundane activities with which we often are involved make it difficult to stay engaged. And even we ourselves, wouldn't we love to be more than we are? Our shortcomings, limitations, and failures are more at times than we can bear.

It ought to be no surprise, really, that given our desire for the bigger-than-life, we look for God to be bigger than life as well. Fill up the big screen. Cause the earth to shake, seas to swell, sweep in larger than life and carry out the spectacular—like a divine superman. Now there's a god to get our attention, one to set our senses a-humming, one we won't miss.

When I was considering a vocation in the ministry, I regularly prayed, "Lord give me a sign. A big sign. A sign I won't miss, so I'll know for sure that I should do this." The picture I had in my mind for some odd reason was a bolt of lightning cracking in front of my car as I drove down the New Jersey Turnpike. Whether it's praying for direction in our lives, or for the threatened life of one we love, or for the future of a community that feels tenuous, we would really like God to be spectacular, carry things off in a big way.

And yet the God we are given is the one who kneels down in front of his friends, wash basin filled with water, towel in hand. He gently reaches out and takes hold of the hot, dry, dirty feet of one after another who has walked with him from lakeside to Jerusalem. Our God pours water so that it runs between bruised toes and over cracked heels. He rigorously dries each foot. The only sounds are of water splashing, people breathing, maybe a surprised gasp or two. No booming soundtrack in the background.

Only the noise of Peter's protests break into Jesus' activity. Peter, too, wants a god who does big, big things. Even after all his time with Jesus—watching Jesus heal the sick, feed the hungry—he is still looking for something grandiose, larger-than-life. God crashing in, upsetting the political apple cart, filling up the Jerusalem screen. Inviting the disciples to share in his power in Jerusalem.

We can hear Peter's longing for that power when he says to Jesus, "You will never wash my feet." Not my feet, Lord. I know what you are here for and this is not it. Don't challenge my clear understanding of who you are, who you yet might be, by wrapping a towel around my feet.

It is hard for us to let go of well-loved pictures and expectations of God. We stubbornly cling to hopes that God will come crashing into our just-to-size life and do the mind-blowing, set-the-neighbors-to-talking kind of activity. Jesus picks up all of that and more in Peter's voice. He hears the fear and the longing. And rather than get impatient with Peter, put him down for his misguided longings, Jesus says very reasonably, "Unless I wash you, you have no share with me" (John 9:8*b*). That is, unless I am welcomed into your life as I really am, you cannot be part of my life and ministry.

A statement of promise through and through—promise that if Jesus does wash Peter, if Jesus is welcomed into Peter's life as a servant, he will be inextricably linked with Jesus. Peter will be bound to Jesus and to Jesus' ministry. The space opened by releasing all those larger-than-life expectations of Jesus will be filled with the knowledge and love of Jesus, who takes on the ordinary and the mundane and blesses them.

To have a share in Jesus is to be with Jesus in the midst of the gentle, the quiet, the just life-sized and to be blessed. Peter hears the promise and, true to form, can't hold back. Once resistant, now exuberant, he cries out, "Lord, not my feet only but also my hands and my head!" (v. 9). Something in this promise awakens his dulled senses, shakes loose his longing for a bigger-than-life God. Peter is invited again to see and hear who Jesus really is: God, who enters quietly, lifts up tired and dirty feet, runs cool water over the dried and cracked places. This promise literally propels Peter out to be one of the great preachers and teachers of the early church, witnessing to God who bends down and washes the feet of those who are worn out at the end of a day's journey.

This promise is ours, too. Jesus comes quietly, ambles into our lives as though coming in from the road at the end of the day, invites us to sit down, and offers to wash our weary feet, to handle them with care. This cleansing washes away the disappointment we carry about our just life-sized lives. It tunes our senses to the simple, the gentle, the mundane in the world around us and blesses us. Blesses us because Jesus enters the ordinary stuff of our lives, and comes as a servant, for us and for the world. No earth-shaking uproar, more like a subtle reawakening. Rejuvenated, cleansed by this wash, we can't help being propelled out—inviting the weary to sit down, offering a little cool water for their tired feet, loving them as Jesus loves us. Amen.

SUGGESTIONS FOR WORSHIP

Call to Worship (adapted from Psalm 116)

LEADER: I love you O God, for you have heard my voice and my supplication.

PEOPLE: **You have inclined your ear to me, I will call on you as long as I live.**

LEADER: You have delivered my soul from death, my eyes from tears, my feet from stumbling.

PEOPLE: **I am your servant. I offer you thanksgiving and call on your name. Praise be to God!**

Prayer of Confession

(In unison.) Gracious and loving God, you have created us and all that exists. You have given us lives that are full to overflowing.

Forgive us when we close our eyes to your gift. Forgive us when we treat your gift as something small and meaningless. Open our eyes so that we may see you at work in the smallest events in our lives. Touch the closed places in our hearts so that we may rejoice at your presence in the ordinary in this world. Bless us, O God. Make us a blessing to others. Amen.

Benediction

God loves us! Let us go into the world as God's disciples, loving one another. Amen.

Good Friday

Mary Alice Mulligan

Isaiah 52:13–53:12: The suffering of the Lord's servant who is crushed, yet exalted. He bears human sins for us.

Psalm 22: The one threatened with destruction calls to God for salvation, finally confident that deliverance will come. God is to be praised forever.

Hebrews 4:14-16; 5:7-9: Jesus, our great high priest, is like us, but sinless. He is the source of our salvation.

John 18:1–19:42: The Passion of Jesus, according to John. The events are central for the life of the church.

REFLECTIONS

A Good Friday service at noon used to be standard fare in many churches, but now attendants could well be limited to the diehards and the few who are available for midday activities (who, by the way, may be the unemployed and rejected, ones desperate for a word of hope). The question of the day is, Why did Jesus die? How one answers that question tells the congregation about God and prepares them for the reversal of the resurrection.

Vague atonement theories float around most congregations: stupid Adam and Eve ruining God's plan (which makes God a victim of human sin and the incarnation an afterthought), or Jesus as our substitute (which makes Jesus a willing payment to a rigid, unmerciful accountant-God). A helpful alternative to these theories is the substitutionary atonement theory of David Buttrick, which keeps the merciful will of Jesus Christ at one with the will of God. Buttrick's theory rests on the belief that God wills to be with humanity. God is mercy, always extending to us. Jesus comes as God-with-us, speaking God's word and revealing God in his actions. The nature of God is self-sacrificing, so Jesus is at one with that nature. The crucifixion shows the unity of the *nature* and *action* of God, which is suffering mercy.

In the crucifixion, we see our own complicity, for Jesus is condemned for challenging the unmerciful, unholy power structures of society, the very structures we daily reinforce. The writer of Revelation expounds: We whore after Babylon. As a result of living in ways so perverted from the truth, we should die, not as a divine punishment, but as a natural result. Our sin should have killed us. But instead, Christ dies in mercy for us. He is our substitute. (See David Buttrick, *The Mystery and the Passion: A Homiletic Reading of the Biblical Traditions* [Minneapolis: Augsburg Fortress, 1992], 222-227.)

We are all guilty, yet even at our most evil, God's mercy surrounds us. When we think of the hammer in our own hands poised over the hand of Jesus held to the cross, we have to be reminded that Jesus loves and forgives us. Before the deed is done, we are pardoned. How else could we call it "Good Friday"?

A SERMON BRIEF

The chancel screen at Emmanuel Episcopal Church includes a wood carving of the crucifixion. The cross is centered and lifted up, so people must pass beneath it on their way to receive Communion. Jesus is stretched out on the cross, giving up his spirit, breathing his last. The final moment of the passion, frozen in time. No matter what the liturgical calendar says, at the chancel rail it is always Good Friday afternoon. Always Jesus hangs there. Sometimes the congregants almost seem to duck as they pass under, lest some blood drip on them. An eternal moment. Always happening. Today we need to look.

In Jesus, God comes to us. God wants to be with us, no matter what. So God shows up. Like a mother who watches her child through a window in the isolation ward. The sicker the child is, the more determined the mother becomes to get in. Without attention to personal threat, she does whatever is necessary to get to her child—break hospital rules, con the nurse, risk catching a fatal illness.

God is like the relentless mother, always wanting to get to us. Understanding God's eternal craving to be with us clarifies the coming of Jesus Christ as part of God's eternal plan. From the foundation of the earth, our Lord Jesus Christ was planned, long before the divine breath first filled human lungs with life. So Jesus comes, the incarnation, the presence of God, right into our life, as a human being.

Amazing, isn't it, the Lord Almighty coming right among us? And if that isn't enough, Jesus mingles with the worst of us. We never heard of his dining at the country club. Instead, Jesus always seems to be in the seediest situations, with the most distasteful folks. And the worst part is that all too often we identify ourselves in the crowd: as people who have just lied their way out of some ugly situation at work or set up house with someone we know won't be around even through the summer. Right in the middle of the worst of us is where God seems to like to be. The incarnation of God comes right where we are.

So no wonder guilt clings to us today. We all feel the shame. If we let our eyes dart around the room, the space seems bigger than usual. Almost hollow. Look at our chancel. The altar is stripped. No flowers. No banners.

And look at us. Today's congregation is as quiet as a room of fifth graders when the principal asks how the window got broken. We feel the cloud over us. Any one of us could report for the group. We feel bad. Just a bit ago, our eyes were mostly cast down when we sang, "Were you there when they crucified my Lord?" Even though the death of Jesus occurred centuries before we were born, we suspect the answer must somehow be, "Yes, we *were* there when they crucified him." None of us can imagine hurting anyone, much less our Lord, but still we feel responsible for his death. After all, his ideas push too hard, demand rigorous changes, threaten the very heart of our political structures and our comfortable religion, too.

No wonder he gets himself killed. We know the rules society sets up. In junior high, we called it survival of the fittest—not just in the jungle, but in our too-human lives. We might laugh when we shrug and say, "Big fish eat little fish," but we know the rule: "The ruthless succeed. Nice people never really get ahead." And the ones who challenge the way society works find themselves pushed aside or worse. All around us, people get riled up if someone like Jesus comes in, demanding sacrificial change, condemning the way we've always done things, acting as if he has a special one-man communication system with God Almighty.

No wonder we sense ourselves in the furious crowd. After all, he threatens the rules we follow so comfortably. We feel bad about it, but nonetheless, in our own hands we can feel the hammer, the nails, the blood. The day reeks of death. We look in the mirror, we identify with the bad guys at the crucifixion: the cut-throat lackeys of the government and the misguided religious fanatics. We all feel heavy with guilt today. Shame is on us.

But look. On the cross you see God. In the cold form of the tortured Jesus, you see God. You probably don't want to look. After the screams of the crowd and the blows of the hammer, there is only silence. The stillness of the frozen moment probably makes you want to look away in disgust and shame. But look. Stand still and consider the cross. The crucifixion frozen in time, as if caught in the eye of an eternal hurricane, with the screaming chaos of total destruction momentarily stopped. Everything good seems smashed to shambles.

Look closer. At the quiet heart of the storm, you see God's very being. In the act of Jesus hanging helpless on the cross, you see the truth. Jesus is synchronized with the will of God, who so loved the world that the worst conceivable thing could happen, and it could be a divine gift. The incarnation of God willingly gives himself in suffering mercy to the world. So you see God best in Jesus, hanging limp and lifeless, for the nature of God is love that suffers all for you, even because of you.

God is absolute, self-giving love. No exaggeration, the Lord of the universe would die for you. When you look to the cross, you discover, beyond your wildest imaginings, you are loved. You are divinely accepted and forgiven, in God's suffering love. For the mercy of God long preceded your sin, even the most grievous. The cross reveals the truth of divine mercy. On the cross, you see God.

So we find ourselves frozen into the scene of Good Friday. Huddling in the shadow, we know the stain of sin on our own hands. Above us, on the cross we see the murdered, silent form of Jesus Christ. Look! The cross holds the undying love of God for us.

SUGGESTIONS FOR WORSHIP

Call to Worship

LEADER: Who will come to worship when we focus on the crucifixion?

PEOPLE: When the closest disciples have fled in terror, who will gather at the foot of the cross?

LEADER: A few will gather and witness to the love of God, poured out for the world.

PEOPLE: **We will come to hear the story again, to witness the death of our Savior, and to worship.**

Prayer of Confession

You are the one, holy God, who first breathed life into human beings. By your will we learn and grow. Yet we confess we act as if we created ourselves and filled our own lungs with life. We spend our days in selfish abandon, lusting after pleasure and success. The idea of laying down our lives for others is ludicrous to us. We are often unwilling to make the smallest sacrifice for others. Forgive our selfish devotion. Deepen our understanding of the love of Jesus Christ, and help us show your love to others. In the name of the crucified one. Amen.

Assurance of Pardon

Scripture reveals that while we were yet God's enemies, Christ died for all. This day of crucifixion, remember: Not by your own deeds, but by the unfailing mercy of God, you are forgiven.

Benediction

Go forth. You have seen the love of God on the cross. Let your lives show forth the divine gift of love to others. And may the unrelenting presence of God fill you with peace. Amen.

Easter Day

Mary Alice Mulligan

Isaiah 25:6-9: The salvation of God is promised for all peoples.

Psalm 118:1-2, 14-25: A song of praise for God's victory.

1 Corinthians 15:1-11: Paul passes on the tradition he received concerning the death, resurrection, and appearances of Jesus Christ.

John 20:1-18: The morning appearance of the resurrected Christ to Mary Magdalene, who testifies to the others.

REFLECTIONS

Every year as I prepare to write the Easter sermon, I remember my Methodist colleague who overheard a choir member reporting to someone who had missed the early service: "The service was good, but the sermon was just the same old Easter crap."

If we expect our congregations to experience the explosive victory of God, we must feel the excitement ourselves. Our sermons dare not be "same-ol', same-ol'." We must figure out the driving joy that propelled Mary back to the disciples to proclaim, "I have seen the Lord!" God has turned the universe on its head. The great enemy, death itself, has been defeated. Jesus Christ, who was stone-cold dead, has burst forth from the grave, alive. Once we touch that joy, we will have the energy necessary to proclaim, "Christ is risen!"

A SERMON BRIEF

An Easter painting by David Gregory shows Mary at the empty tomb, absolutely distraught. Isn't it enough her Lord has been murdered? Now they've stolen his body! She is slumped over in despair, leaning against the cave entrance as if the world has done its worst and she cannot go on. But over her shoulder, walking toward her in the cool, garden morning, is the risen Christ. She doesn't yet see him, but she is in his presence nonetheless. Curiously, the painting is entitled "Go tell" At the lowest moments, we are in the presence of Christ, who is sending us to "Go tell."

We want to hang on to Jesus. We can hardly imagine letting go of our Lord, if we could just get him within our reach. If we could just touch him, we would never let go. So we understand Mary on this first Easter morning, absolutely understand her, so overjoyed to see her teacher alive. She had watched them execute Jesus. She knew he was dead. No wonder she wants to throw her arms around him, grab him, and hang on forever.

Thus we can also feel the slice of his words: "Do not hold on to me." Mary expects everything to go back to normal, but no such luck. Jesus will no longer be the wandering preacher-rabbi. The past is over. Mary cannot hold on to the Jesus who used to sit on the hillside and teach the multitudes how to live.

We understand her desire to have things return to the predictable, normal past. She is like an inexperienced child on the playground monkey bars, swinging out to reach the second rung. But when she grabs it, she is afraid to let go of the first rung. Dangling there, suspended in space, terrified of the unknown future, she lets go. But if she is going to move forward, she has to let go.

Letting go of the past is difficult for all of us. Some of us remember when the men's Sunday school class alone had more than a hundred members. Wonderful memories! How easy to get caught up in wanting the congregation to return to those glory days, but we can't hold on to the past, either. We can appreciate the past, learn from it, honor it, but the old life is not coming back.

Like Mary in the Easter morning garden, we find ourselves clinging to the old ways of understanding Jesus and what he is doing with his church. Our eyes aren't fully trained to see Jesus as he comes to us now. We just want to hang on to the Jesus we know.

But the resurrected Christ is going to God. Christ has arisen on his way to God. The language is peculiar, isn't it? What does he mean, "I am ascending to God?" He means that something completely new has happened at the tomb where they laid the lifeless body of Jesus. Resurrection.

Be very clear. Resurrection is not mere resuscitation. Breath did not just suddenly start back up in the old, beaten-up body of Jesus. His old body could never support the new life. No, resurrection is *a new creation*. Jesus Christ, the resurrected Lord, will never die again. He is no longer merely Jesus.

Look! The disciples can touch the risen Christ. He eats a piece of fish in their presence, but he is able to pass through locked doors. You begin to understand the idea of dying with a corruptible body and being raised incorruptible. Jesus can speak and hear others, yet in the midst of people, he may be hidden or he may let them recognize him. The *resurrected* Christ. The one to whom cruel humanity did its worst, does not merely breathe again. He lives! Never to die again. Jesus Christ has let death do its worst, and he lives. Death itself has been swallowed up in God's victory. So the stabbing pain of death has been dulled, because death has been shown to be powerless against God's will.

Jesus is the Christ of God, who has struck down death, and even now rises to God. He is the prince of God's new order: King of kings and Lord of all creation. How can you even stay in your pews on Easter Sunday morning? The resurrected Christ is on his way to God.

But there is more amazing good news: We experience the resurrected presence of Christ here. The resurrected Christ is among us. We might call it one of the miracles of the faith: Christ's spirit is present in our gathering together. Jesus Christ is the resurrected and exalted Lord, yet somehow he is present here when we worship. We can sense the risen Christ among us, encompassing us, and making *us* something new. And when we gather together to celebrate the resurrection, we move together into the very presence of God's realm. Can we believe it?

When we worship together, there is the power of the resurrected Christ among us. The church is the fellowship of the resurrection. In fact, if we aren't connected to the resurrected Christ, we are individuals, alone.

Will Campbell, a minister who dropped out of organized Christianity some time back, still performs an occasional pastoral duty—a wedding now and again—but always out on his Tennessee farm, in the middle of nowhere. Someone asked him what he missed about being a congregation's pastor, and he said, "I miss the people singing on the river bank when I baptize someone."

Of course, when a person is baptized, the community needs to be there. We experience the presence of the resurrected Christ when our friends are baptized. The candidates and I do not go before God alone. No. The whole church participates. The Christian faith is group faith. We act together, and we are saved together. The resurrected Christ is among us.

No wonder, then, we are told to "Go tell!" We are expected to tell the good news of Jesus Christ. Some might say we are to share the wealth. When we find folk whose faith falters (and they are around us daily), who have gotten to the place where they are convinced the faith doesn't matter, we are directed to tell them the Lord of the universe has defeated the powers of death. They may believe life is temporary, but life is eternal. Death is temporary. Their faith does matter, because it is the truth. (Then, of course, invite them to church.)

Other times, when we find folk crushed by circumstances of life, we are directed to tell them that Jesus, too, was crushed to the ground and had his life snuffed out. The crushed of the earth are God's special, chosen ones. But we can't expect people to believe such words. We have to tell them how precious they are to God by our actions. To go tell the oppressed, we have to become servants.

We all know the story of a Christian health worker, nursing untouchable dying people in grisly conditions, and the proper church lady, handkerchief over her nose, who gasps, "I wouldn't do that for a million dollars." The worker replies, "Neither would I." The Christian message is more precious than money, and more powerful. Christ is risen. We must share the wealth. No wonder we are told to "go tell!" others. Easter morning is the best day of the year. We get to decorate the sanctuary, sing the greatest hymns, hear the ancient story, participate in Christian baptism, and celebrate God's finest victory, when death itself is conquered. The risen Christ is among us, bringing us into God's realm. Alleluia! Christ is risen indeed!

SUGGESTIONS FOR WORSHIP

Call to Worship

LEADER: Alleluia! Christ is risen!
PEOPLE: **The Lord is risen indeed! Alleluia!**

Prayer of Confession

Almighty God, we praise you for the glory of this day, when we celebrate the victory of life over death. Jesus Christ has risen, in spite of all the power of evil to stop him. This is joyous news. Yet we confess the enthusiasm of the morning may be fleeting, as the certainty of Easter dwindles day by day. We are unsure whether we believe out of conviction or habit. Forgive our duplicity. Renew our faith. Strengthen our service. We pray in the name of the risen Christ. Amen.

Assurance of Pardon

Followers of Jesus Christ, our Lord burst forth from death alive. Leave your sins behind and live. In the name of our resurrected Savior, you are forgiven.

Benediction

Christ has risen, precious friends. Go forth in his power, witnessing to his mercy this day and always. And may the joy of Easter morning remain in your hearts forever.

Second Sunday of Easter

Anna Carter Florence

Acts 4:32-35: The group of early believers lives in unity and shares their possessions.

Psalm 133: A very brief psalm about how blessed it is to live together in unity.

1 John 1:1–2:2: The word of life: in God is light, and in God is no darkness at all.

John 20:19-31: Jesus appears to the disciples; Thomas doubts and later comes to believe.

REFLECTIONS

The possibilities for preaching today's Gospel reading are mind-boggling. One could do a nice word study, for instance, focusing on the distinction between "believing" and "believing *into*" (closer to the Greek). But what catches my attention is the chronology of John's Easter account: first, the discovery of the empty tomb; second, Jesus' appearance to Mary, who is still weeping at the tomb when the disciples have long since left; third, Jesus' appearance to the disciples in their locked room; and fourth, Jesus' appearance to Thomas, the last holdout. It's a striking progression. The power of God seeps into human time and gradually we come to see it, but it means waking up from the groggy half-sleep of *this* world, with all its limited ways of seeing and being. Notice how incredibly persistent God is: if people can't or won't believe what is before them, God puts it to them another way. It's as if God knows that we all come to faith in very different ways.

As a woman, I treasure this sort of openness and acceptance. Without it, I could place no confidence in the times in which I have felt addressed or at least interrupted by the Spirit. I couldn't bind myself to the community of faith, unafraid of our differences, nor could I go to these texts freely, unafraid of what might come out of our exchange. Because the truth is that sometimes I am like Mary, running light-footed and sure and bursting with news, and sometimes I am like Thomas, seething and pouting and up for a fight. The truth is that God keeps putting this stunning good news to me and to you in myriad ways, knowing that our ability to truly hear and receive it can waver. That, for me, is the point of this text's placement in the lectionary: one week after the high of Easter, we're up and swinging, ready to take out anyone who is fool enough to believe such fairy stories as these.

God doesn't even blink. So Thomas won't believe until he sees, huh? Okay, let's take it from the top, if he really wants to. Only this time, let him have it between the eyes.

A SERMON BRIEF

I have always been grateful to Thomas. He gives the rest of us a break. It's almost as if John knew that angels and miracles won't do it for everyone; some of us can't see our way in unless—as the current expression has it—we're *keepin' it real.*

My family and I discovered this in a big way when we lived for five years at a boarding school in the hills of northern New Jersey. For those of you unfamiliar with boarding-school life, imagine a youth-group retreat that goes on for about nine months straight, and you aren't far off. My husband was the chaplain, responsible for the spiritual life of four hundred largely unchurched high school students. One of his duties was to conduct weekly chapel and vespers services. For those of you unfamiliar with boarding-school chapel, imagine a worship service in which attendance is taken and you get in trouble for not showing up. Now imagine trying to preach to four hundred adolescents who *have* shown up, under duress, but would *all* rather be someplace else. It took my husband about five minutes to realize that everything he'd learned about preaching in seminary and in the parish wasn't going to help much in this setting. He had to ask new questions and look for new forms, because these kids had never heard of Moses and had no patience for platitudes. But they *were* interested in the big picture; they *were* interested in questions of faith. The important thing was *keepin' it real*, which could be the mantra for adolescence and which isn't a bad way to go, no matter how old you are.

Keepin' it real. I think you could make a good case for Thomas being the youngest disciple in the group—say, about eighteen years old. If you think about it, it makes sense. Why wouldn't Jesus want a member of the youth group on his team? Why wouldn't he want a little representation and diversity through the life cycle? If the resurrection stories tell us nothing else, they make it clear that people come to the risen Christ in many different ways. Some of us only need an empty tomb and a few folded linens. Some of us need the risen Christ to come to us on our own turf, because although we wish we could face the empty tomb, we cannot. And some of us can't take anyone else's word for it; we have to experience it ourselves. We have to get as close as we can to the nails and the danger and the tumble with our own mortality, because there is this drive deep within us to risk our childhood and find out what is on the other side.

That's Thomas. He's *keepin' it real.* And he doesn't care, frankly, what the other disciples saw in that upper room when he was out doing God knows what, because unless he sees it with his own eyes, he can't count himself one of them. Believing has to do with a*ction,* doesn't it? It has to do with following, with drinking the same cup your leader drank, with casting your nets as wide as you can, with *just doing it,* not with turning all passive and docile about the junk the world hands down to you! Thomas's cry is the cry of youth everywhere: "Unless I see the mark of the nails in his hands, and put my finger in the mark of the nails and my hand in his side, *I will not believe*" (John 20:25, emphasis added).

It's a direct challenge, and the beautiful thing about it is that Jesus doesn't judge him for it. He lets the boy—if we can call him that—have his way. Jesus understands that there is a time in life when we have to rage and doubt and question and taunt those we love and admire most, because we have to test the strength of the world they offer us. We have to test our own strength. We have to know if we, too, are worthy to follow, all the way to the cross. We have to know if we can take to the streets for resurrection, if that's a cause worth living and dying for, because we're not about blind obedience, we're about *keepin' it real.*

Thomas does make his confession. "My Lord and my God!" he breathes, when his hands have touched that body. "Have you believed because you have seen me?" Jesus asks him. "Blessed are those who have not seen and yet have come to believe" (John 20:28-29).

116

Some church folk see Jesus' words as a pointed rebuke of Thomas's behavior, but I am not one of them. I think Jesus is just saying what we already know: Sometimes we believe because we have seen, and sometimes we believe even when we have not. The grace in this passage is that we are allowed to do both things. We can be passionate and stormy, shaking our fists at the sky. We can be serene and contented, saying our evening prayers. We can live our whole lives without ever once needing proof, or we can set off on a pilgrimage to find it; it doesn't matter. Whether we are smack in the middle of adolescence or deep into maturity, the risen Christ finds a way to meet us. He finds a way to make our wounds his own.

My husband's students loved Thomas. Why wouldn't they? He spoke their language. He stood up to God. And God accepted it; God even blessed him for it. Imagine a God who tolerates your questions, these students said! Imagine a God who isn't threatened by doubts! Imagine a God who understands that even though you have this tradition, you still might need a little concrete evidence in your life! Oh, yes. If you're *keepin' it real*, they said, you can do it with a God like this. You can do it like Thomas.

Thanks be to God.

SUGGESTIONS FOR WORSHIP

Call to Worship

LEADER: How beautiful it is when God's children live together in unity!

PEOPLE: **It is like precious oil poured upon our heads; it is like the morning dew from the mountain of God.**

LEADER: Sisters and brothers, let us be of one heart and soul.

PEOPLE: **Let us share what we have and shout what we know: Christ is risen!**

ALL: **Allelulia! Christ is risen!**

Prayer of Confession

O God of light, we confess that we have turned from your truth once again. We have settled for foolishness when the path of wisdom seemed long. We have hoarded your gifts when we might have shared them freely. We have snapped with impatience when we might have spoken in love. We have let broken things lie. Forgive us, O God. Turn your light upon us, so that we may see clearly. Give us time to amend what we are, and courage to become what we might be, through the grace and power which are yours alone. We pray in the name of Christ. Amen.

Assurance of Pardon

Hear the good news! God is light. God is truth. And despite all that we are and all that we are not, God makes of us a new creation. Sisters and brothers, believe the gospel: in Jesus Christ, we are forgiven. Amen.

Benediction

The grace of God pour down upon your heads,
The love of God surround you like the mountains,
The peace of God fill all your days with light.
Go and serve the Lord,
And may the spirit of Christ be with you. Amen.

Third Sunday of Easter

Valerie Brown-Troutt and Yvette Flunder

Acts 3:12-19: After healing a crippled man, Peter preaches the gospel to those gathered in Solomon's portico.

Psalm 4: The psalmist prays for deliverance and then asserts trust in God alone. "You have put gladness in my heart . . . I will both lie down and sleep in peace."

1 John 3:1-7: Believers are called children of God and are told they will one day be pure as God is pure.

Luke 24:36*b*-48: Jesus appears to the disciples as they are gathered together in Jerusalem, and they mistake him for a ghost. He shows them his hands and feet, eats fish in their presence, and tells them they are witnesses to the events foretold in the scriptures about the Messiah.

REFLECTIONS

I am blessed and encouraged by the depiction of weakness and the empowerment of weak ones in this Gospel narrative, which describes the last events of Jesus before his ascension. One of Jesus' final acts on the earth locates him on the road to Emmaus (defined as "earnest longing"). Emmanuel ("with us is God") comes near and close to two believers who talk about everything that has happened. Their downcast faces bespeak their disappointment and their longing for Jesus. Preoccupied with their broken hopes for a messiah who would redeem Israel from its enemies, they have walked away from Jerusalem—away from the fellowship of believers there. Jesus calls them "foolish" and "slow of heart to believe all that the prophets have declared" (Luke 24:25).

It is to these that Jesus comes, breaks bread, and leaves his final witness: to ordinary people who were slow to believe, disappointed, and headed in the wrong direction. It was these ordinary ones who took the message of encouragement to the eleven whom Jesus found behind locked doors.

A SERMON BRIEF
I Want Jesus to Walk with Me

In our culture of privacy rights for the individual, the notion of having other people knowing more than our social security numbers, driver's license numbers, and ID numbers makes us very suspicious and uncomfortable and sometimes leaves us feeling violated. There is an unspoken code of silence in our culture that says privacy is good, silence is golden, and talking too much about oneself or others is taboo. You can easily be branded a big mouth if you talk too much.

In our high-crime, if-you-see-don't-tell society, just about everyone is seeking a low profile. People may be assaulted on crowded public streets, and no one stops to help, no one says a word. Parents are teaching their children that it is good not to tell. Children are learning the old adage, "Silence is golden."

But is silence always golden?

In our Gospel reading this morning, Jesus told the disciples who were locked behind doors that they were to be his witnesses. To those who were troubled, startled, frightened, and doubtful because they thought they had seen a ghost, the resurrected Lord appeared, standing in their midst, speaking peace.

To be a witness is to see and testify, to tell. And the world is in need of a witness—someone who has seen and can verbally testify about Jesus—someone who will break the silence.

Has anyone seen Jesus? Has anyone witnessed the power of his reality in the world? What things can we tell that others cannot tell?

In our biblical text Jesus goes out of his way to remind his followers of what they have heard and seen. He encourages them to look at his body; he eats before and with them; he opens their understanding; he blesses them, and he ascends before them into heaven. This group who earlier had been terrified, frightened, and disbelieving now become worshipers, filled with wonder and great joy.

Notice that Jesus recognized and worked around the limitations of the disciples. He modified his approach for their understanding.

What did it take for them to become witnesses? First, they had to believe that Jesus was who he said he was. Jesus said to the disciples,

"It is I myself" (Luke 24:39). The scriptures say that whoever seeks God must believe first that God is (Heb. 11:6).

Second, the disciples needed to eat with Jesus. Jesus loved to dine. There is something about sharing a common meal that elicits fellowship. And Jesus meets us where we are hungry or able to consume, relate, and digest. Twice in this chapter of John's Gospel we see that there is no understanding of who Jesus is without this type of communion around a meal.

Third, the disciples needed to understand who Jesus was in relation to their own Hebrew Scriptures. Jesus opened their minds and hearts so that they could understand their own scriptures more fully.

And finally, Jesus blessed them and promised power from on high. "I am sending upon you what my Father promised," he said, "so stay here in the city until you have been clothed with power from on high" (Luke 24:49).

God recognizes and works with our limitations by modifying his approach for our understanding and witness. The African American spiritual "I Want Jesus to Walk with Me" sings of a people who knew that "all along the pilgrim journey the Lord would walk with me." This same Lord walks in "my trials, my sorrows." This same Lord not only walks, but also holds our hands as we go. Songwriter Danibelle Hall says that God chooses and uses "Ordinary People."

I am encouraged today that Jesus chose not only to appear to the disciples in the upper room, but also to go outside of the city of Jerusalem to walk and talk with people on the margins and on the road to Emmaus. People headed in the wrong direction, Jesus chose to be his witnesses.

I am encouraged today that Jesus told these people that they would be his witnesses. Jesus is a God of encouragement and empowerment. This is prophetic empowerment. God is saying today, "You shall be my witnesses. Lift your head up! Be encouraged for I yet live!"

Go, tell it on the mountain! Go, tell it on the mountain, over the hills, and everywhere that Jesus Christ is alive! Go, tell it on the mountain, over the hills, and everywhere that Jesus Christ saves, heals, and restores. Go, tell it on the mountain, over the hills, and everywhere that Jesus Christ is able to deliver and set the captives free. Go, tell it on the mountain!

Jesus is yet walking on the dusty road of Emmaus—walking together with us to help us confront our disappointments, sort out our desires, aspirations, and dreams. It is Jesus who is yet meeting us on the road of Emmaus, when we have gone away from the strength of Christian fellowship into the withdrawal of self-pity and self-reliance.

It is Jesus who is yet picking us up and turning us around. Hallelujah! It is Jesus who is yet opening our understanding, enabling us to handle and present the scriptures to those who have not believed, in joy and in wonder, in the goodness of the Lord.

Jesus is yet appearing in our midst when we are behind locked doors. John's Gospel tells us the doors were locked for fear of the Jews. Today, our doors are often locked because of fear related to religion, sexism, and classism.

Just look around at the witnesses of our history and see Jesus speaking through other voices. I hear the witness of Sojourner Truth seemingly saying, "Peace be unto you my sister-daughter. Tell the truth for freedom's sake when they doubt who you say you are. Don't be afraid of your femininity, bear it in truth to your enemy's shame."

We are free today because Jesus said, "Peace be with you." We have power today because Jesus sent power from on high. And we can continually be witnesses because we have known the remission of sins in Jesus Christ our Lord. As pardoned people, let us rejoice and praise God with great joy.

SUGGESTIONS FOR WORSHIP

Prayer

God, you who are worth talking about, we worship you.

God, you who are worth talking about, give us tongues of freedom, so that we might declare your goodness among us and others.

God, you who are worth talking about, send us where witnesses are needed.

God, you who are worth talking about, help us to ever be reminded of the things we have heard, handled, and seen in this life.

God, you who are worth talking about, you with nail-scarred hands, stretch out your hands of tender mercy and show us again the wounds that save and heal us.

God, you who are worth talking about, pick us up and turn us around, placing our feet on solid ground.

God, you who are worth talking about, your name is worthy to be praised.

God, you who are worth talking about, we will be your witnesses. Amen.

Benediction

As you leave, my sisters and brothers, walk knowing that Jesus is with you.

As you leave, my sisters and brothers, talk the talk that believes that what Jesus says is true.

As you leave, my sisters and brothers, share with one another and witness hope. Amen.

Fourth Sunday of Easter

Catherine Erskine Boileau

Acts 4:5-12: Peter and John refuse to cease witnessing to the living Christ.

Psalm 23: The beloved song celebrating God's ongoing presence in our lives as shepherd.

1 John 3:16-24: The definition of love: that we lay down our lives for others.

John 10:11-18: Jesus, the Good Shepherd, is unafraid to lay down his life for his sheep.

REFLECTIONS

Today is Mother's Day. Today will be joyous for some, but bittersweet for countless others who mourn the loss of family members, struggle with estranged or blended families, or grieve the loss of the children who never were. Even families who come with children in hand will ask as you step into the pulpit, does the church have anything relevant to say to the bewildering vocation of parenting in the new millennium? To deny the joy, confusion, and pain of this day is to miss an opportunity for the gospel to powerfully address our culture. But care is needed in preaching. A sermon extolling Beaver Cleaver's mother as the epitome of womanhood oppresses the childless woman as well as the mother struggling with daycare, custody battles, and the like. We as preachers need to prayerfully and creatively seek metaphors in keeping with the realities of life for mothers today.

As I read today's texts celebrating God's ongoing presence in our lives as shepherd, I was struck by the danger that lurks in all of these texts. One issue that rests in the hearts of mothers this Mother's Day is undeniably the violence of our culture. The shepherd texts acknowledge that we live in a violent world. The true shepherd is one who stands against the wolves and gives his or her life for the sake of the sheep. While John 10 is clearly about the unique role of Jesus in the community of faith, 1 John warns that Jesus' followers should likewise stand vigilant with staff in hand, willing to lay down our lives for the sheep God entrusts to us. The metaphor of shepherd can be a powerful challenge to all God's people to stand in the full power of our shepherd against the wolves who continue to prowl to this day.

A SERMON BRIEF

Someone to Watch Over Me

Some images of scriptures become so familiar that we are in danger of missing their power. Whenever I hear those comforting words of Psalm 23, my mind is instantly filled with a painting of a lush, emerald pasture with contentedly munching sheep. The deep blue skies are filled with white fluffy clouds; a gentle, flowing stream tiptoes nearby. And there on the hillside, leaning serenely against a grove of trees, is a shepherd, eyes alert and smiling, fondly watching his sheep.

At first glance, it would seem that the image of Jesus as shepherd has little to do with our lives as mothers in the twenty-first century. Particularly for those of us with children still at home, that comforting promise of peaceful green pastures and quiet still waters vanishes in the face of carpools and soccer practice and getting everybody out the door in the morning. Mother's Day cards would have us believe that our vocation as mothers consists of serenely rocking a drowsy, contented child; but those of us on active duty know it is much more about the arguments about homework, searching for that missing library book, and your fourteen-year-old's tears about curfews. We might identify more with the psalm if the psalmist had written that our shepherd guides us down clear highways or leads us beside children who sleep through the night. Maybe the image of Jesus as shepherd has simply lost the power of its punch in our brimful lives as mothers and women. Or has it?

The first thing I hear as I read these texts anew is that being a shepherd is a dangerous job. Danger? In that serene, peaceful setting? Psalm 23 acknowledges that enemies are a part of life. In Acts, the apostles witness under threat of their lives. First John warns that we who follow Jesus should stand ready to lay down our lives. Perhaps these shepherd texts have an edge that we often miss in our nostalgia for greener pastures.

In John 10, the threat to the sheep comes in the form of wolves. Wolves are predators. Sometimes they travel in packs, sometimes as loners, but their instinct is to attack the weakest, frailest member of the flock. I am beginning to listen very closely to this shepherd named Jesus. For although I know the four-footed variety of wolf is endangered, there is no scarcity of wolves in my life. There are the wolves, predators, who stealthily make their way into our communities, smuggling drugs to our children. There are the corporate wolves who market new products that cause damage to our bodies, and wolves who make money without remorse while they destroy the environment. There are wolves who bring violence into our communities. And those predators are getting younger all the time. Keep talking, Jesus. You have my attention now.

And then Jesus says something else that hits home. He says that there is a vast difference between a hireling and a shepherd, a tension that we have always sensed but rarely verbalized. The hireling cares little for names or faces, just the paycheck. As long as the paycheck is enough to compensate for the boredom and the inconvenience and the mess, the hireling remains. At the first sign of trouble, however, the hireling flees, leaving the sheep to fend for themselves. What paycheck could ever be enough to compensate for losing your life?

That's the difference. The true shepherd is only revealed in a moment of crisis. When the wolves appear, the hireling flees, leaving the sheep to fend for themselves. But not a shepherd. A shepherd doesn't think about his or her safety at the moment of crisis; the shepherd's only concern is for the sheep. Have you ever seen a mother when her children are threatened? Jesus says it's not enough to know their names or dress them in Gymboree outfits and make sure they make it to soccer practice. It's not enough to tuck them in and kiss them goodnight and teach them to say their prayers. Being a shepherd means you are always on vigil, scanning the horizon, watching for the wolves. Being a shepherd means the rod and staff are always in your hand. A shepherd is exactly what those tender young lambs need when they live out in a violent world overflowing with danger. I think I'm beginning to understand.

Things haven't changed much. Hirelings abound in our day, just as they did in the first century. There are hirelings in public office whom we expect to watch over our nation and society, who in the end care only about reelection or writing their memoirs. Hirelings are those individuals whom you meet daily—at the fast-food place or the Social Security office or the hospital—who aren't willing to exert themselves one inch beyond what their job descriptions require, even if it means helping out another human being. We have heard terrifying stories of daycare workers and others entrusted with our children's care who were hirelings after all. Even within the church, there are hirelings who stealthily creep into our pulpits, people whom we expect to be shepherds to the flock of God but in the moment of truth break our hearts. We learn too late that they also have abandoned the sheep. But every once in awhile, a true shepherd emerges.

In March of 1998 in Jonesboro, Arkansas, two school children, ages eleven and thirteen, took violent revenge on their classmates. After triggering a fire alarm, they sat with hunting rifles, waiting for their classmates to come out. One by one those two young children took aim and fired at those they intended to kill. In the midst of the chaos and confusion, a young teacher named Shannon Wright saw that the guns were pointing at a young student named Emma. In a split second, Shannon covered the child with her body. Emma lived. Shannon died. In that moment of crisis, a true shepherd was revealed.

I can't read Shannon's story without tears. As a mother who is soon to release my children to the public school system, I thank God for shepherds like Shannon whom God inspires to watch and protect our children in our absence. Thank God for those neighbors who look out the window at those latchkey kids and take a special interest in their lives. Thank God for those stepmoms who become real moms to their blended families and for those grandmothers who raise those grandchildren as their own. Thank God for those shepherds who keep vigil in the neighborhood, who will not remain silent when they see wolves on the horizon. As a mother, I pray that God will continue to raise up shepherds for our community and our nation. And I pray that God will raise up shepherds to watch over a little five-year-old boy named Zane, who on this Mother's Day is without his mother, because Shannon gave her life for the sheep.

Maybe a shepherd is exactly what we need in the twenty-first century. Because of Shannon's witness, I will never again watch that bumbling teenager in the fast-food restaurant without tenderly remembering that he is someone's son, and a sheep in my fold. I will claim the time, energy, and boldness to speak out against those actions that hurt or demoralize children, whether the harm comes from the senate, the church, or the school board. I will keep my eyes open for the sheep in my life who are lost or wounded, whether or not I gave them birth. And when I feel lost or bewildered or at risk of being devoured by the wolves, I will look to Jesus, the one unfailing shepherd of the flock. For just as Shannon laid down her life for Emma, Jesus laid down his life for me. I will find my refreshment at his overflowing table, even in the presence of my enemies. God's rod and staff shall be my armor. And on those days when we most need a shepherd, I will look for Jesus to come, especially to places like Jonesboro, Arkansas. I will raise my children in faith, because Jesus our Good Shepherd could never abandon his sheep. I know, because Jesus sent Shannon.

SUGGESTIONS FOR WORSHIP

Call to Worship

LEADER: The cry of the wolf surrounds us, but we who belong to God shall not fear.
PEOPLE: For God is our shepherd.
LEADER: When we hunger in the midst of abundance, God moves us to green pastures.
PEOPLE: In our anxiety-ridden lives, God leads us to still waters.
LEADER: God is our past, our present, our future.
PEOPLE: Surely goodness and mercy have followed us.
LEADER: In God's house we will dwell forever.
ALL: Sing songs of praise to the redeemer of our souls.

Prayer of Confession

As a shepherd lovingly tends the sheep, you have embraced us, O God. When we were lost in the crevices of self-deception and sin, you left heaven to seek us. When we abandoned the fold for that which did not satisfy, your rod held us back from destruction. When death threatened to tear us from your fold, you gave your life in our place. Forgive us, O Lord, for the countless ways we have wandered from your side this week. Forgive us, our loving shepherd, for pretending that we did not know it was you when you called. Heal our restless hearts, convert our faithless wills, and renew our broken spirits, that we might walk with you in paths of righteousness and dwell in your house forever. Amen.

Assurance of Pardon

If our hearts condemn us, God is greater than our hearts. Return to your loving shepherd, and God will warmly receive you back into the fold.

Benediction

Go forth in joy, for you are God's beloved sheep. Go forth in power, for greater is God in you, than the one in the world. Go forth in love, for that which God has shared with you is meant to be shared with others. Amen.

Fifth Sunday of Easter

Adele Stiles Resmer

Acts 8:26-40: Philip proclaims "the good news about Jesus" to an Ethiopian eunuch who is reading scripture. In response to the good news, the eunuch asks to be baptized by Philip.

Psalm 22:25-31: This is a psalm of lamentation that ends with statements of trust that "the poor shall eat and be satisfied" and all nations will bow down to praise God.

1 John 4:7-21: The writer affirms that "there is no fear in love" and commands us to love others because God has shown love for us in Jesus Christ.

John 15:1-8: Jesus declares that he is the true vine and God is the vine grower who prunes us, the branches, so that we will bear more fruit. By abiding in Jesus we will bear much fruit and glorify God.

REFLECTIONS

It might be tempting to shy away from the 1 John text because the assertion that "there is no fear in love" at first sounds so contrary to much of our experience. Furthermore, it can be interpreted legalistically—that is, it can become a should: we should not have fear as we love, and we should love others. The way I want to approach this text for preaching is to acknowledge the coexistence of love and fear for us and then bring that reality into contact with the promise that our experience of God's love in Jesus Christ creates the possibility of fearless love that does reach out to others.

A SERMON BRIEF

In the movie *As Good As It Gets*, Carol is a waitress with a young son who has crippling allergies and asthma. He cannot run and play with other children. He easily wheezes and gets so short of breath that he is confined to his bed. Carol has taken her son to the emergency room so many times she can't remember; no one is able to cure his worsening condition. Her days are weighed down with worry. When she comes in the door from work, her first question is, "How is he?" If she cannot see or hear him right away, her face tightens with anxiety, her eyes widen with fear; surely something terrible has happened. Carol's love for her son becomes indistinguishable from her fear for his life. When quirky Melvin, a regular in the restaurant where she works, makes a crack about her son, her face and eyes freeze. She verbally strikes out at Melvin. Love and fear are completely entangled on her face and in her life.

The writer of 1 John states, "There is no fear in love" (4:18), but like Carol we know better. We know that fear and love live together quite naturally. Our love for our parents shares space with fear when they start throwing things or become chillingly quiet. We want to be close to them but get away from them all at the same time. Love for a partner lives side by side with fear that one day we will lose him or her. We want to share ourselves, but we don't want the hurt that will come with separation. Love for our children competes with fear that we cannot protect them, that they are vulnerable. We want to support their growth and independence, but we don't want them to be hurt. Our deepest loves indeed seem naturally to cozy up to fear.

In fact, our loves seem to be the source of some of our deepest fears. It's the deep connections we make with others, the risks involved in such relationships, the potential for loss that runs through them all that provides the fertilizer for fear, aiding and abetting fear's growth and flowering. So we often find ourselves loving in ever so guarded, careful ways. Our love is gift-wrapped in anxiety, and we place all kinds of conditions on our love. We tell ourselves we're being wise, even realistic—that this is a mature and knowing love. Truth is, underneath it all, it is love surrounded by fear, shaped by fear.

Yet 1 John affirms, "There is no fear in love," and in this affirmation suggests that there is a reality that is different from our usual experience of things, affirms that there is such a thing as love unfettered by fear. We can't help asking, how is this possible? And 1 John gives us an important clue when it says, "Perfect love casts out fear"

(4:18). Perfect love—who of us knows anything about perfect love? Where do we turn to learn something about this elusive reality? What does it look like?

In Flannery O'Connor's short story, "A Good Man Is Hard to Find," an old, scattered woman, along with her son, daughter-in-law, and two grandchildren, travel down a deserted dirt road to find the home she thinks she remembers as a young girl. Their car crashes, and they all climb out. Another car pulls over, and three men get out. The old woman recognizes one of them as a criminal called Misfit, and she screams. Misfit's two friends lead the rest of the family into the woods and shoot them. Meanwhile, Misfit talks to the old woman about how he wishes that he'd been there to see if Jesus really rose from the dead. If he'd seen it himself, maybe he'd be different. As he goes on, the old woman sees his face twist as if he's about to cry, and she murmurs, "Why you're one of my babies, you're one of my own children." As she reaches out to touch him, he jumps back and shoots her.

This scattered old woman is what perfect love looks like. Indeed, for O'Connor, she is the presence of Christ on the side of the road. O'Connor knows that it is only Jesus Christ who is our picture of perfect love—Jesus who is God's gift to a people whose loves and fears get all entangled, at times to a murderous end. Jesus washes Judas's feet and loves him while Judas actively betrays him to the authorities. Jesus heals the sick and feeds the hungry as others ponder how to get rid of him. Jesus feeds and washes his disciples on the edge of Jerusalem, where he will meet his death. From the cross Jesus cries out, "Father forgive them. . . ." Risen, he brings peace to disciples hovering in fear behind closed doors.

Jesus is God's healing and transforming presence, fearless in loving people into a new and life-giving relationship with God and with one another. He is fearless in his ministry to transform lives and loves crippled by fear. In Jesus, we see what perfect love looks like. Perfect love recognizes a connection with another, even one who is a murderous criminal. It reaches out to others even in the face of danger. It loves even as the smell of death is wafting in the air.

This fearless, perfect love of Jesus reaches out to us. It surrounds us in the water that washes us in baptism; it fills us in the bread and wine that feeds us. It lifts us up in prayers and conversation offered for our encouragement and renewal. It heals us in the life-affirming touch of another, in the selfless act of another, in the rapt attention of another. We can turn away from these expressions of love as did the criminal, Misfit. Or we can allow ourselves to be transformed, stepping into lives where fear's fierce grip is loosened.

In the film *As Good As It Gets,* Carol hesitantly agrees to accompany the eccentric Melvin and an artist named Simon on a trip to see Simon's parents. Simon is an artist who has been severely beaten by men robbing his apartment, he is estranged from the parents he is on his way to visit because of his homosexuality, and he is broke. Simon watches people, observes them carefully for lengths of time. He believes he can uncover the humanity of any person with such observation. On their trip, Simon turns his attentive eye to Carol. He watches her closely, observes the beauty that pushes past the brown circles under her eyes, the compassion that softens her face, the fire that lights up her eyes. He tells her what he sees and he sketches what he sees. Carol is transformed by being deeply seen. Her experience with Simon cracks open what has been contained by fear. It allows her to open up to quirky Melvin, to rejoice in the returning health of her son, to love with less fear.

When we are transformed by even a fleeting experience of perfect love, we are cracked open a bit—the fear that surrounds our loves is shaken loose. We are able to grow in our ability to love more perfectly those we claim as family and those we view as strangers, even enemies. We can reach out with a fearless love, willing to risk because we are known in the perfect love of Jesus.

SUGGESTIONS FOR WORSHIP

Call to Worship (adapted from Psalm 22)

LEADER: All the ends of the earth shall remember and turn to you O God,
PEOPLE: **and all the families of the nations shall worship before you.**
LEADER: Future generations will be told about you O God,
PEOPLE: **and proclaim your deliverance to a people yet unborn, declaring that you have done it.**

Prayer of Confession

Gracious God, we come before you full of fear: fear for ourselves, for those we know and love, and for the whole world. We protect ourselves and turn away from those around us. Transform us with the healing power of your love, O God. Loosen fear's grip on us so that we can be more fully who you have created us to be, your expression of love in the world. Amen.

Assurance of Pardon

Hear the good news: God's love casts out fear! Rejoice and shout aloud of God's goodness. Amen.

Benediction

Set free by God's love, let us go into the world, loving our sisters and brothers fearlessly. Amen.

Sixth Sunday of Easter

Dawn Ottoni Wilhelm

Acts 10:44-48: To the astonishment of the circumcised believers, the gift of the Holy Spirit is poured out on the Gentiles.

Psalm 98: Through every instrument and sounding board, through all of nature and humankind, a new and joyful song of God's impending justice is to be sung throughout the world.

1 John 5:1-6: We show our love for God and one another through obedience to God's commandments.

John 15:9-17: The commandment to love one another as God in Christ loves us is accompanied by a new relationship between Jesus and his disciples. No longer servants, we are friends of Christ because God shares freely with us and commands us to love and bear the good fruits of loving service.

REFLECTIONS

Few of us would deny that friendship is a gift of God. But most of us would like to ignore the fact that friendship requires vulnerability, hard work, and a willingness to share with others. These are the qualities Jesus shows us in his life and ministry, and according to John 15, our Lord calls us to love one another in the same way. Just as God shares with us fully and intimately through Jesus Christ, we are also asked to offer ourselves to others in love. When I consider that Jesus is willing to pledge his friendship to those who, in a few short chapters, will betray, deny, and abandon him, I am moved to believe that we, too, may learn to be more generous in our love for others.

135

A SERMON BRIEF

I remember the hot summer day my childhood friend Fran and I decided to seal our friendship by the most sacred ritual we had heard of. We sat on Fran's front steps with a sharp pin in our hands, taking turns as we tried to prick the skin of our palms in hopes of drawing blood, then rubbing our hands together in a handshake that would seal our friendship for life. One of us would take a jab and then the other would try, but it wasn't as easy as we thought. We sat on that cement step for what seemed like hours with the sun beating down on our sweaty palms, brushing our hair out of our eyes as we kept jabbing half-heartedly at our hands. After so much poking away with that pin we were frustrated and fidgety and finally decided that if blood was worth sharing then surely saliva was just as good. We spit in our palms and slapped a quick high five before launching off on our bikes.

Strange and wonderful are the things friends share together: matinees and bike rides, music and sleep-overs, fishing and joking, jewelry and clothing, stories and secrets, and street hockey and sandwiches. All the little and great things that make a relationship a friendship and keep a friend for life.

Friendship must surely be one of God's greatest gifts to us. It is what God wants for us; and according to the fifteenth chapter of John's Gospel, God wants friendships not only *for* us but also *with* us: "I do not call you servants any longer, because the servant does not know what the master is doing; but I have called you friends, because I have made known to you everything that I have heard from my Father" (v. 15).

You know me, Jesus is saying. You know with whom I eat and the people with whom I contend; you know what makes me angry and you know those for whom I have mercy; you've heard my parables and learned my prayers. That's how it is with friends. They share what is most important with one another. And if you want to be my friend, Jesus is saying, then you've got to share my love, too.

According to John's Gospel, Jesus shared many things freely with the disciples, and he repeatedly made known to them his close relationship with God, whom he called "Father." "I am in the Father and the Father is in me," Jesus said, and "I have made known to you everything that I have heard from my Father" (14:10, 15:15). Earlier in John's Gospel, it is also clear that Jesus not only knows the will of the Father, but also knows the hearts of the disciples. He knows that one of his closest friends will betray him (13:21), another will deny him (13:38), and the rest will abandon him. Yet he calls them his friends, and though it must have cut like a knife, he kept on loving and kept on sharing. Right to the last drop.

Love one another. It sounds so very good but is so very difficult to do. It's often difficult to share ourselves with others, to be vulnerable to their rejection and uncertain of their response.

A few months after I moved to Huntingdon, Pennsylvania, to serve as pastor of the Stone Church of the Brethren, I was rushing out the door to make a visit when I saw a member of my congregation walking along the road with a briefcase in hand. When I pulled over to offer a ride he happily agreed, so I drove him to his meeting then zipped down the road, later than ever. I put the pedal to the metal and began blasting my way down Cold Spring Road when I heard a siren and saw the flashing red lights of a state patrol car signaling me to pull over.

Flushed with anger at myself, I rolled down the window as the officer approached our old Honda. "Do you know how fast you were going, ma'am?" In the brief exchange that ensued, I tried to explain that I was late for a visit, but he had already pulled out his ticket pad and asked for my license. As he headed back to the patrol car to make a license search, I slunk down in my seat. But anger soon gave way to another sensation as I saw across the road a woman approaching my car. It was Helen, another member of my congregation, who lived just across from where I'd stopped. I felt my cheeks turn blood red with embarrassment. There I was, her new pastor, pulled over for speeding.

"Are you all right?" she asked out of genuine concern. "Is anything wrong? Are you sick?" I cleared my throat and sat up straight. "Only with embarrassment," I confessed. The officer returned to my car. "Oh, officer," Helen said with more sincerity and enthusiasm than I could muster at the moment, "she would never hurt anyone. She's our pastor."

"Uh huh," said the patrolman, unmoved by her testimony. "And she was speeding, ma'am. Here's your ticket. Don't do it again."

As Helen returned to her home and I crawled down the road to my visit, I thought to myself that I was in for it now. I could read the headlines of tomorrow's *Daily News:* "New Woman Pastor Caught Endangering Lives Through Reckless Driving—Congregation Considers Taking a Vote of Confidence."

But I never heard another word about it the next day. Or the next. And the following Sunday when Helen and her husband came through the greeting line after worship with grins on their faces, they both gave me a wink and said the words every delinquent pastor longs to hear: "Don't worry. We won't tell." And they never did. They didn't judge or reject me, either: they accepted me, lead foot and all. And because of that, I found myself able to trust others in the church all the more.

Love and friendship are risky because we are ever vulnerable to others, but Jesus Christ shows us a love that is willing to risk rejection and able to carry us through our failures and fears. Love one another. It's not a choice but a commandment—the toughest and greatest one of all. Tough because there are times when our friendship will be rejected, our loyalties betrayed, and love will prick and pierce our lives in the painful giving of ourselves to others. And great because the love of God is an inexhaustible source of joy, able to bear fruit in our lives that will last an eternity. May the one who befriends us all love you always. Friends, love one another.

SUGGESTIONS FOR WORSHIP

Call to Worship

ONE: Come sing a new song to the Lord.

ALL: **There is a song of love as old as the ages that we are in need of learning anew each and every day.**

ONE: Come rest your fears and steady your hearts.

ALL: **The love of God frees us to offer ourselves in love to God and one another.**

ONE: Come abide in Christ's love and obey God's command.

ALL: **We are blessed to be called friends of God and able to bear fruit that will last forever.**

Prayer of Confession

(In unison.) Great Lord and friend of all, we confess that the love you have shared with us we have only half-heartedly shared with others. Because we are quick to offer criticism, we are awkward in offering praise. Because we are eager to share our opinions, we are slow to discern your potential. Because of the demands we place on ourselves, we have forgotten your command to love one another. Bless us with your generous Spirit so that we may love one another as you have loved us, through life and death to newness of life. Through Jesus Christ we pray. Amen.

Assurance of Pardon

Because of God's great love for us, our sins are forgiven and we are friends of Christ.

Be filled with joy, free to love, and gifted to bear fruits worthy of repentance.

Benediction

May the love of God bless you as you love one another.

May the friendship of Christ strengthen you to be a friend of Christ to others.

Ascension Day

Dawn Ottoni Wilhelm

Acts 1:1-11: In the second Lukan account of the ascension of Christ, the disciples witness Jesus being lifted up to heaven after he tells them of the Holy Spirit who is to come.

Psalm 47: As the Lord ascends to his throne, the psalmist invites us to join the celebration.

Ephesians 1:15-23: In his prayer for the church at Ephesus, the writer speaks of the empowerment of the disciples and the power of Christ who has ascended to heaven.

Luke 24:44-53: Before his final departure from earth, Jesus opens the minds of the disciples to understand the meaning of scripture, then promises them power from on high.

REFLECTIONS

I am struck by the fact that Luke is the only Gospel writer to describe the physical ascension of the Lord. More than a theological explanation for Jesus' departure before the coming of the Holy Spirit, Luke offers us an image of Christ that is both transcendent and empowering. Just as remarkable is the surprising response of the disciples, who are neither fearful nor concerned, but joyful as they return to Jerusalem, worshiping and blessing God in the Temple. In reading Luke's account I have the sense that when Jesus rose to heaven he somehow lifted us all a little higher, reminding us to set our sights on the kingdom of heaven even as we keep our feet firmly planted on earth.

A SERMON BRIEF

The last time Jesus walked among his disciples on earth, I imagine him standing a little higher than usual. Following the resurrection, he revealed himself to his closest followers. According to Luke, he met two of them on the road to Emmaus, where he joined them for a fish fry; and then he returned to Jerusalem, where he showed up behind closed doors and opened his disciples' minds as he interpreted holy scripture for them. Then he offered his parting message, words that were simple and strong, intended to motivate the disciples to set their sights a little higher in the days to come: "I am sending upon you what my Father promised; so stay here in the city until you have been clothed with power from on high" (24:49).

Power from on high. Jesus was setting his eyes toward heaven, and with his feet barely touching the ground, he knew that the strength his disciples needed could not be found within themselves or in one another or from anywhere on earth, but elsewhere: from on high. Look up, Jesus seemed to be saying. Look a little higher. Look beyond yourselves. Then he lifted his hands in blessing as he was carried away to heaven.

It's an amazing scene: mysterious, incomprehensible, even unbelievable for many of us. The ascension of Christ stretches our faith as well as our imaginations. I would not have blamed the disciples if they had been filled to overflowing with ambivalence and fear, awe and anxiety. It was a scene of glory but also one of abandonment; a time of wonder and of sadness.

But sadness was the farthest thing from the disciples' experience as Jesus ascended to heaven. In fact, Luke tells us that they were joyful and downright festive. There isn't a downcast eye among them. They don't look back longingly to the good old days in Galilee but move on to Jerusalem and the Temple, where they bless God continually and wait for power from on high.

When Jesus ascended to heaven, it was as if God wanted to remind us that as we trudge around with heavy hearts and leaden feet here on earth, we are yet headed for heaven. Jesus, who was among the most grounded people to walk the earth, also showed us the way to move beyond it. While on earth he gave us parables of the kingdom of heaven; while he healed our earthly wounds he promised us heavenly power. He was Jesus and Christ, God's anointed king who is able to lift us all higher than we would ever be able to lift ourselves.

One Monday morning, shortly after I had returned to my full-time pastoral responsibilities following the birth of our third child, a man stopped by my office to speak with me about my sermon of the day before. He was not a member of my congregation, but was a respected leader in his own right. I welcomed his visit, and we sat down in my study together as he began asking me questions about our worship service and about my sermon in particular. I listened and responded to the best of my ability; and it seemed that he was joking with me a bit, poking fun at my stories and illustrations, until he finally landed his punchline, saying that he'd never heard such ridiculous drivel before. My greatest offense, he said, was in my opening story, a story about my family of origin sitting around the poker table discussing their ailments and afflictions. What I had intended as a humorous illustration for prodding my congregation to ponder their own experiences of suffering, my visitor felt was terribly profane—a trivialization of the gospel of Jesus Christ.

Without a single word of encouragement, he finally left; and I felt as if I'd been pummeled and left beaten in a ditch. Worst of all was my fear that I had indeed trivialized the gospel. I decided to seek the perspective of a parishioner who was supportive of me but, more important, would not shy away from giving me an honest appraisal of my sermon. After talking with Harriet, I began to feel once again as though my stories were helpful. It was as if someone had lifted me out of the ditch.

But I still felt strangely troubled by the whole thing—until I was visiting another member of our congregation in the hospital. Mavis and her husband greeted me with a smile and invited me to sit for a while. When her husband made a colorful comment about the hospital staff, Mavis said, "Now, don't you listen to him. You must learn to let some things go in one ear and out the other. But then you know all about that, don't you? You must hear all kinds of things." She had my full attention as she continued, "But I love to listen to you. Especially your stories. They have a way of lifting my spirit. And I remember," Mavis continued, "one time long ago you told a story about your family playing poker. I said to myself, if she can find Jesus at a poker table, then I can find him anywhere, too." Mavis didn't know it, of course, but her words lifted me higher than any amount of sermon analysis could ever have done.

God's power is there for us all the time. We have God's blessing in every moment we lift one another up in Christ, a little higher than we could on our own. When the first disciples saw Jesus lifted up to assume the throne of God, they saw what we all need to remember: that God has the power to lift us beyond ourselves, away from our selfish preoccupations, and out of the painful entanglement of our fears. With power from on high, God lifts us all a little higher and into the kingdom of heaven.

SUGGESTIONS FOR WORSHIP

Call to Worship

ONE: Come worship the Lord, who is here among us, yet is beyond our greatest imaginings.

ALL: **Ours is the God of mystery and revelation, who searches our hearts and knows our minds.**

ONE: The Christ who walked among us is also the Lord who rose above us.

ALL: **The king of the earth sits on a heavenly throne, calling us to serve this world even as we seek the next.**

ONE: The blessing of Christ is upon us and over us to clothe us with power and reveal our hidden glory.

ALL: **We gather to worship the Lord our God as we offer ourselves in service to Christ.**

Prayer of Confession

(In unison.) Almighty and ever-loving God, we confess that our lives fall short of your glory revealed to us in Jesus Christ. When you move among us, calling us to attend to the gentle stirring of your will, we clutter our lives with noise and distractions. When you offer us depth of meaning and an eternity to know you, we skate along the surface of our lives, hurrying frantically from one task to another. When you raise your hand in blessing, we turn our backs in denial, unwilling to see the suffering of others whom we are blessed to serve. By your great love and mercy, help us when our zeal is short-lived and our vision is nearsighted. When we are satisfied with what has been and have stopped searching for what might be, lift us out of our selfish preoccupations to set our sights on you. We pray in the name of Jesus Christ, our Lord. Amen.

Assurance of Pardon

Through Jesus Christ
our sins are forgiven
and our strength is renewed.
Rise with Christ
and walk in newness of life.

Benediction

May the Lord who is over and above all
be within and around you.
May God raise you up to live with Christ in heaven
even as you serve one another on earth.

Seventh Sunday of Easter

Margaret K. Schwarzer

Acts 1:15-17, 21-26: Peter announces that the apostolic position left empty by Judas must be filled; so "they cast lots . . . and the lot fell on Matthias."

Psalm 1: "Happy are those who do not follow the advice of the wicked."

1 John 5:9-13: The writer of 1 John discusses the divine nature of Christ: "God gave us eternal life, and this life is in his Son."

John 17:6-19: Jesus prays for his disciples as he prepares himself for crucifixion. Christ's deepest prayer is that his disciples will find his "joy made complete in themselves."

REFLECTIONS

Elizabeth Barrett Browning, one of the past century's most-respected poets, had an eye for seeing grace in ordinary times. "Earth's crammed with heaven," she wrote, "and every common bush [is] afire with God." Many women preachers carry on Barrett Browning's legacy; we choose to point out the common bush aflame with God. We tend to be less reluctant than our male counterparts to acknowledge the godliness of the intimate gesture or the everyday routine. I have heard women preach wonderful sermons about endless phone calls with their closest friends, keen discussions shared with three-year-olds, or the intimacy of deathbed conversations. Earth is crammed with heaven, and as we find our voices, we have an urgency to share that truth with our congregations.

When I read the lectionary texts for this Sunday, a single phrase from John's Gospel captured my attention: "I speak these things in the world so that [my disciples] may have my joy made complete in themselves" (John 17:13). I do not usually preach on a single phrase of scripture. Often the most important tensions emerge from the juxtaposition of our three readings and psalm, and I like to reflect upon those tensions with the congregation. However, in this case, preaching on that single phrase seemed to be the right thing to do. What kind of joy did Jesus have, and how or when do we know ourselves to be filled with it? That is the question I set for myself in this sermon. In the process of answering it, I looked for common bushes aflame with God.

A SERMON BRIEF

When I was a deacon in Washington, D.C., I worked in a vibrant and innovative church on Connecticut Avenue named Saint Margaret's. One of our church's matriarchs was married to one of the church's patriarchs; at seventy-four and seventy-six, they were a matched set of liberal, dynamic Episcopalians who worked in soup kitchens and raised money to support our mission in Honduras. But their passion was environmentalism. They focused 80 percent of their retirement hours around the needs of our planet and our city.

Every Saturday morning they toured the Dupont Circle neighborhood, collecting cans and bottles that could be recycled. Usually, they began their search around eight o'clock in the morning, but on one November morning a Capitol Hill rally they planned to attend required them to look through Dupont Circle at a much earlier hour. When they arrived to check out the eight or nine trash barrels around the circle, there were already five homeless men ahead of them. The men were beginning to search through the trash barrels for remnants of food. Since the first one to look into each barrel had the best chance of finding breakfast, a pecking order was being established.

As our parishioners moved toward the first trash barrel, two homeless men who were still waiting to begin their search looked up and seemed startled. Dressed up in their "hunting-for-cans" clothes—old baggy pants, worn jackets and sneakers—husband and wife were quite a sight. The youngest homeless man gestured to them to step ahead of him into the midpoint of the line, but our two parishioners declined. Wanting to follow the street etiquette of "first come, first serve," they insisted on waiting their turn. So, one-by-one, five homeless men and Sarah and James began moving around the circle, hunching over trash barrels, sifting through paper and soiled foam containers, each hunting for particular fare.

By the time Sarah and James got to the fourth trash container, they were finding a few bottles and cans and putting them in a garbage bag. When they got to the fifth trash barrel, they noticed the same silent young man circling back toward them. He stopped in front of their trash barrel and looked directly into James's face. "There's a McDonald's up the street," he said. "Go buy your old lady a cup of coffee." As he said it, he crushed a crumpled dollar bill into James's hand. The young man didn't wait for a reply; he just spun around on his heels and off he went—still searching out breakfast.

Now, that young man may not have known that he was following in Jesus' footsteps, but he was. "This is my commandment," said Jesus, "that you love one another as I have loved you" (John 15:12).

It didn't take Sarah or James long to figure out that they had been mistaken for two old homeless people. Their worn clothes had made them look impoverished. In gratitude for the young man's gift, they went to McDonald's and split a cup of coffee between them. It made them late to the rally, but they knew their lateness had a blessing in it. Greater love hath no one than to hand over his money to two perfect strangers. It's quite a thing for a man to do, especially when he has nothing to start with.

In this morning's Gospel reading, Jesus says, "I speak these things in the world so that [my disciples] may have my joy made complete in themselves" (John 17:13). And last week, in John's Gospel text, we heard Jesus say something very similar: "I have said these things to you so that my joy may be in you, and that your joy may be complete" (John 15:11). Neither passage defines what Christ's joy is, or what it might mean to live with Christ's joy fulfilled in us, but both statements invite us to consider Christ's hopes for us carefully.

First, it seems clear that the kind of joy Jesus is speaking about is not the obvious satisfaction that comes from buying a new car or a new TV; his joy isn't about possessing something. Neither is this joy the kind of happiness that comes as a consequence of living; it isn't a joy that results from a beautiful sunset or a shared walk on the beach. Those are true joys, but those joys are a consequence of our dwelling on a beautiful planet. Christ's joy seems to have something to do with how we choose to love one another; it seems to be the by-product of loving genuinely and selflessly, in the way Christ has loved us.

I'd like to suggest that the joy that Christ hopes will fill us is like

147

the strange kind of joy that shows up in our story of trash barrels and McDonald's coffee. The nameless young man did a loving deed, but his offering cost him something. His generosity must have brought him the joy true kindness brings, but his joy came on an empty stomach. His wishing another well meant that he had less for himself. That kind of joy requires stamina. That joy also points us toward the self-sacrificing nature of Christ's love for us. Whether or not he thought of Christ, that homeless man chose an experience of joy over the reasonable conclusion that he had nothing to offer the old couple. He lost his dollar, but he found a vibrant part of his own heart. And the joy he set in motion did not limit itself to the boundaries of his own life. Sarah and James, so used to giving and providing for others, had a rare chance to know the joy that comes from receiving a very precious gift. An extraordinary gift. A gift beyond price. They got to experience what extravagant generosity feels like; they got a small taste of heaven. Who would have guessed that heaven tastes like McDonald's coffee?

We grow in our likeness to Christ when we choose love over security, or recognize heaven in a cup of coffee. To give freely what is needed, without resentment or expectation, pulls us into the very heart of the gospel. When we love our neighbor in this way, we become Christ's friends. We experience Christ's joy. To accept a costly gift gratefully, without fawning or pretense, also pulls us into the very heart of the gospel. When we let ourselves be loved by our neighbors in this way, we fuel ourselves with that love; we store up that love in readiness for the time it will be called forth from us. To give a precious gift freely or to receive a precious gift freely produces the joy that shoots down into the marrow of our bones; it brings us a sense of heaven.

Christ loved perfectly, and we love imperfectly, but that is not supposed to stop us from the attempt. When we're children, we grow in Christ's joy by giving someone else the last candy in the box or the last piece of chocolate cake. As adults, we grow in Christ's joy when we find ourselves at an important gathering and spend time speaking with someone who is feeling awkward or shy. We grow in his joy when we are kind to someone who appears not to have a friend in the world. Whether we are children or adults, we grow in Christ as we become more generous.

If our generosity is what helps us grow into our identity in Christ, it should not be surprising to discover that some anthropologists and sociologists declare that our generosity is what sets us apart from the animals on our planet. Some anthropologists, including Dr. Richard Leakey, tell us that it was not our brains but our selflessness and generosity that first separated us from other animals during evolution's unfolding. Dr. Leakey states that "what truly separates [us] from . . . the chimps and baboons . . . was not . . . intelligence, but . . . generosity." He goes on to say that "sharing, not hunting or gathering as such is what makes us human" (David Albert Farmer and Edwina Hunter, eds., *And Blessed Is She: Sermons by Women* [Valley Forge, Pa.: Judson Press, 1994], 103). We began to be human because our ancestors chose to share their food and their skills.

Our generosity makes us human. It's a thought worth considering. So often we are led to believe that it is our intelligence and our competitive talents that chart our evolutionary success. "Survival of the fittest" is Darwin's hypothesis, but the well-respected Dr. Leakey responds with a "survival of the generous" theory. Is it competition or generosity that ensures that we survive? Which one ensures that we thrive? However we are inclined to answer, we know that Jesus believes that more than competition is required to make us human: "This is my commandment," he says, "that you love one another as I have loved you" (John 15:12).

Christ's prayer for each of us is that we continue to expand our capacity for self-giving love. One way to practice that self-giving is to give our dollars or our time, not for the acquisition of stereo systems or cars, but for the promotion of neighborly well-being. Buy the box of cookies when the Girl Scout asks; buy groceries for a hungry family; teach someone to read. We can start out small and see where love calls us to go next. We can begin with a cup of coffee.

Within the next month, may we each find the opportunity to welcome a stranger, so that Christ's joy may be in us, and a stranger's joy may be full. Amen.

SUGGESTIONS FOR WORSHIP

Call to Worship (adapted from Psalm 1)

LEADER: Happy are the ones who have not walked in the counsel of the wicked.
They are like trees planted by streams of water.
They bear fruit in due season,
and their leaves do not wither.

PEOPLE: Happy are the ones who have not walked in the
            counsel of the wicked.
            They are like trees planted by streams of water.
            They bear fruit in due season,
            and their leaves do not wither.
            Everything they do shall prosper.

Prayer of Confession

(In unison.) Lord, we come to you knowing the smallness of our own hearts. We do those things we ought not to do, and we do not do those things we ought to do. Hear us as we pray aloud, or silently in our hearts, naming those failings we need to confess to you. (A period of silence follows.)

Assurance of Pardon

Hear the good news. Our God is slow to anger and quick to offer mercy. We are forgiven in the name of the Trinity, the sacred one in three, now and forever. Amen.

Closing Prayer

You are gracious, O Lover of souls,
and we are your grateful people;
teach us to love in glad abandon;
teach us to love as Christ loved us.
Let us have an eye for grace,
and a heart for kindnesses.
Let your love for us be in our minds,
and upon our lips, and in our hearts,
for love's sake. Amen.
(Inspired by *The Book of Common Prayer* [New York: The Church Hymnal Corporation and the Seabury Press, 1976], 395.)

Day of Pentecost

Eunjoo Mary Kim

Ezekiel 37:1-14: "I prophesied as he commanded me, and the breath came into them, and they lived, and stood on their feet, a vast multitude."

Psalm 104:24-34, 35b: "When you send forth your spirit, they are created; and you renew the face of the ground."

Acts 2:1-21: "All of them were filled with the Holy Spirit and began to speak in other languages, as the Spirit gave them ability."

John 15:26-27; 16:4b-15: "When the Spirit of truth comes, he will guide you into all the truth; for he will not speak on his own, but will speak whatever he hears, and he will declare to you the things that are to come."

REFLECTIONS

When there is no hope from the human side, God works for our new future through the divine Spirit. When the people of Israel were so desperately hopeless in Babylonian exile that they couldn't imagine God's mercy, God showed Ezekiel a hopeful vision for Israel's future. The vision in which the spirit of God restored lifeless dried bones to a vast living multitude was God's promise to renew the nation.

The life-giving power of the Spirit was also the source of a new spiritual community in the New Testament. The disciples of Jesus who experienced the power of the Holy Spirit in Jerusalem after Jesus' ascension couldn't help proclaiming the good news of God's salvation through Christ Jesus to the world. The Holy Spirit is still working for the renewal of our community, and its life-giving power is experienced in our present context.

A SERMON BRIEF

Have you ever seen a landscape full of skeletons? I suppose some of you may have experienced the Korean or Vietnam War and seen multitudes of dead bodies with your own eyes. Or some of you might have seen the movie *Schindler's List* or *The Killing Fields.* Such movies show us scenes with piles of dead bodies scattered all around.

But what I am talking about is an even more terrifying scene than these. I am referring to the valley of death: a valley in which the bones have been lying around unburied for a long time—bare bones, already picked clean by the vultures, stripped of their skin and flesh and sinews, bleached and dried out by the heat of the day. Thousands of such dried bones cover the whole floor of the valley. Neither a breath of life nor a gleam of hope for life, but only a dreary and gloomy sound of wind fills this area. It is the valley of death. Have you ever seen this?

One day, God called Ezekiel out into a valley that was filled with dried bones. It might have been a battlefield where long ago the Babylonians had defeated the Israelites. We don't know for certain where or what it was. But of Ezekiel, who was standing in the middle of this valley in horror and despair, God asked, "Can these bones live?" Can these dried bones become alive again?

In response to this unexpected question, Ezekiel sidestepped a direct yes or no answer. Instead he responded, "O Lord God, you know." Then God commanded Ezekiel to prophesy to these lifeless bones, "O dry bones . . . I will cause breath to enter you, and you shall live . . . and you shall know that I am the Lord" (37:3, 5, 6).

As soon as Ezekiel finished speaking these words, there was a noise, a rattling sound, and the bones came together, bone to bone. Then flesh appeared on them and skin covered them, and finally breath entered them and they, in fact, came to life and stood up on their feet and finally became a vast living army. The lifeless dry bones became an exceeding great army in God's service!

In Ezekiel's time, Israel seemed as hopeless as these dried bones. The people lived in exile as slaves of the Babylonian empire. Surrounded by a heathen culture and values that were opposed to those of their faith, they felt they couldn't expect God's gracious help because they believed their exile was God's punishment for their sins. They deplored the fact that God had abandoned them and was no longer on their side. Like lifeless dried bones, their spirits had dried up. Their hope was gone. Their future was closed. And it was in the midst of this predicament that God began to give them hope through this vision.

When we desperately experience the dead end and see no hope for our future, God, who is the life-giving Spirit, works for us. The transforming power of the Spirit creates a new life, a new community, and a new world.

We see evidence of God's transforming and life-giving work not only in the story of Ezekiel, but also in the story of the first Pentecost we read this morning from Acts 2. Jesus' disciples and others who confessed him as the Messiah were gathered in one place on the day of Pentecost. Since Jesus had ascended to heaven, they might have felt empty, but instead they devoted themselves to prayer, waiting for the Holy Spirit that Jesus had promised. Suddenly, they felt something strange, like divided tongues of fire accompanied by a violent sound of wind. This phenomenon filled the entire house where they were sitting and rested on each of them. Then something miraculous happened: they began to speak in other languages.

Some of you may imagine that their speaking in tongues might be the same as what some Pentecostal and charismatic churches emphasize these days: uttering mystical words that no one but the Holy Spirit could understand. But their speaking in tongues was different. According to the story, those gathered suddenly began speaking in a variety of languages, which were the native tongues of all those who had come to Jerusalem from other places. "Parthians, Medes, Elamites, and residents of Mesopotamia, Judea and Cappadocia, Pontus and Asia, Phrygia and Pamphylia, Egypt and the parts of Libya belonging to Cyrene, and visitors from Rome, both Jews and proselytes, Cretans and Arabs"—all were able to hear about God's deeds of power in their respective languages (Acts 2:9-11). This was genuine communication through which the gospel was proclaimed to all people.

In the first century, many of those gathered suffered political and economic exploitation at the hands of the Roman Empire. To make matters worse, the Jewish religious leaders' legalistic teaching couldn't help people keep their faith alive in the promises of God. Like bones in the valley of death, their spirits had dried up—without future, without life, and without hope.

Then, in the midst of this valley of death, a miracle happened. A hopeful future was initiated by God; the breath of life came into the people by the spirit of God; and a gleam of hope arose from the new message of the gospel.

Those who experienced the power of the Holy Spirit could not help telling the residents and visitors of Jerusalem in their native languages about God's salvation through Jesus Christ. Their message had power to overturn the valley of death and transform it into the valley of living creatures. The life-giving power of the Spirit renewed the dried spirit of each individual and created a new spiritual community.

The spirit of God is a transforming power that creates a new life, a new community, and a new world.

Have you even seen a valley of dried bones? I think there is one not far from us. For dried bones are found not only in the Bible story or on foreign battlefields, but also here, in the communities where we live and work. Although we live in one of the wealthiest, most stable countries in the world, sometimes we also feel as if our spirits are drying up. A money-oriented secular mentality confuses our purpose in life and makes us lose our way, our future direction. A selfish individualism results in broken relationships with others. Many of us are intolerant of those who come from a different culture or speak a different language, refusing to truly communicate in our multiracial and multicultural society. Even in the church, we force others to learn our language rather than learning theirs, seeking to be understood rather than to understand.

Although called to this community of faith by God, we often experience how difficult it is to be one in Christ. And often we hear the sharp sound of dried bones banging against each other at home, at church, and in our society. In this valley of dried bones, we are stuck. We don't know what to do in order to create a living army in God's service.

Yet our scripture passages for today testify that it is at times when we experience a dead end and see no hope for our future that God, who is the life-giving Spirit, starts to work for us. The life-giving power of the Spirit creates life where there is no life and can bring into being a new community and a new world.

My dear friends, our hope is in God alone. Our community's future is also in God. Let us pray, then, to God. Let us pray with one mind for the presence of God within us, who is the life-giving Spirit.

O come to us, Holy Spirit, and renew our spirits. Amen.

SUGGESTIONS FOR WORSHIP

Call to Worship

Come, let us worship God who is the life-giving Spirit.
Come, let us worship God who is the life-sustaining Spirit.
Come, let us worship God who is the life-transforming Spirit. Amen.

Prayer of Confession

LEADER: God of life, we come before you with lifeless spirits.

PEOPLE: **Forgive our sin and renew our spirits.**

LEADER: God of hope, we come before you with hopeless minds.

PEOPLE: **Forgive our sin and restore our hope.**

LEADER: God of the future, we come before you without a vision for our future.

PEOPLE: **Forgive our sin and create our future in your spirit.**

ALL: **Through Jesus Christ, our savior. Amen.**

Assurance of Pardon
(adapted from Romans 8:22-24)

LEADER: We know that the whole of creation has been groaning in labor pains until now.

PEOPLE: **And not only the creation, but we ourselves, who have the first fruits of the Spirit, groan inwardly while we wait for adoption, the redemption of our bodies.**

LEADER: For in hope we are saved.

PEOPLE: **Thanks be to God!**

Benediction

May the Spirit of truth continue to sustain us, guide our future, and transform us into a living army at God's service. Amen.

Ordinary Time 14 or Proper 9

Elizabeth McGregor Simmons

---

2 Samuel 5:1-5, 9-10: David is anointed king over Israel.

Psalm 48: The glory and strength of the city of Jerusalem are considered and celebrated.

2 Corinthians 12:2-10: The Lord says to Paul, "My grace is sufficient for you, for power is made perfect in weakness."

Mark 6:1-13: Jesus is rejected by the folk of his hometown. He then proceeds to send out disciples with a word of warning that they, too, may be rejected.

REFLECTIONS

Summer is Vacation Bible School time in my church, as I imagine it is in many of yours. Seeking guidance for my presentation to the elementary-age folk who would make a stop at my "Bible Exploration Station," I was thumbing through the curriculum when my roving eye was snagged by the curriculum writer's number-one theological admonition: "Thankful people are happy people."

As I rooted through closets, gathering up robes, sashes, scarves, and sandals for my VBS costume, I couldn't help engaging in some imaginary theological sparring with the curriculum writer. Had the writer ever read the sixth chapter of Mark? I wondered. What would he or she say about the first three stories that Mark 6 contains, stories not about "happy" people, but about rejected people?

A SERMON BRIEF

The Gospel lesson today is about rejection. My hunch is that there is not a person listening to the reading of the text who needs a dictionary to define what rejection is.

Rejection is when you're sitting at the dinner table, bursting with some new morsel of knowledge you savored at school that day. What you learned that day was really neat, you thought, but when you open your mouth to spurt it out with enthusiasm for everyone else to hear, there is a chuckle from the other end of the dinner table where your father is seated. "I was only teasing," your father would protest if you were to tell him how it feels, but it feels like rejection to you.

Rejection is when a friendship that you had grown to count on, a friendship that once meant not only casual chitchat about clothes and children but real heart-to-heart communication about both your lives, turns into phone calls not returned, eyes that evade rather than reveal, and finally the soul-wrenching emptiness of knowing that you're no longer involved in one another's life.

Rejection is going to a meeting, maybe even a meeting at church, really sensing that you have a vision of what the group is to do and be. You make your proposal for the organization of the food pantry. You state the need in the community. You pass out the Xeroxed copies of the proposal to everyone. It's a good idea; you know it. You've done a good job presenting it. And then the person on your right clears his throat and unsheathes his dagger, slashing your proposal into minuscule shreds left to litter the floor as the meeting adjourns.

Rejection layers our lives in these and in a thousand other ways. And it was something that Jesus experienced, too. The rejection that Jesus experienced in this incident took place in his own hometown, among those whom he knew and who knew him best. He scandalized the local folk: his high school band director, his third grade Sunday school teacher, the matronly woman who had baby-sat with him when he was a kid. He looked like the same old Jesus they knew so well, the one who had been so polite and helped his daddy so willingly in the carpenter shop. But what he said when he stood up to preach in the synagogue that day . . . well, it was a little more truth than they were used to or comfortable with, so they rejected what he said. They rejected him.

Mark, who wrote this Gospel, included this story of Jesus' rejection for a reason. He means to say, I believe, that for Jesus and for those who follow him, rejection is inevitable. For Christians who seek to walk in the ways of Christ in every aspect of their lives, rejection is the name of the game.

Jesus, having experienced rejection himself, sought to prepare his disciples for that same kind of experience. He counsels them to travel light and then he doles out explicit instructions about what to do when they are rejected: "If any place will not welcome you and they refuse to hear you, as you leave, shake off the dust that is on your feet as a testimony against them" (Mark 6:11).

So the disciples were counseled to expect rejection as they went about the countryside sowing the seeds of Jesus' liberating word. And if we are faithful, we can expect it, too.

We may whip up our courage to share what faith in Christ means to us with someone else, only to have the person stare back at us blankly. We may write letter after letter to our representatives and senators telling them about how we view health care reform as a matter of simple Christian justice, only for those letters to go unanswered, and to pick up the paper to read of yet another day of wrangling over the issue and our political leaders no closer to a resolution.

We may spend hours with an alcoholic friend, picking him up from a bar when he phones in the middle of the night unable to drive home, sitting with him while arrangements are made to admit him to detox, listening as he tells us he is over the hump, he's making it, only to have the phone jangle three weeks later for an excruciating reprise of the situation.

For Christians, rejection is often the name of the game. If we commit to following Jesus Christ in every aspect of our lives, we can expect rejection.

But we can also expect something more. For the gospel is not ultimately the story of rejection. It is in the end the story of rejection transformed.

The gospel is good news precisely because rejection is, by God's gracious mercy, not the final word. The rejection that Jesus faced here, in his own hometown, at so many other places in his ministry, and in the end, in his death on the cross, is gathered up, overcome, and transformed into the glory of the resurrection. And so for Christians, *rejection* is never the last word. *Rejection transformed* is.

A child, crushed by the laughter of rejection at the dinner table, by God's grace grows up to be a parent who takes care that the words spoken to his children are words of healing, helping, sharing. Rejection transformed.

A friend, even though an adult, "grows up" a little bit through her own experience of rejection to become someone not so eager to control, someone better able both to give and to receive love. Rejection transformed.

A Christian, still stinging from the rejection of his food pantry proposal, goes to church and sees on the Communion table bread and wine, symbols of a body broken and blood spilled, symbols of rejection transformed into signs of love and unity. And after the Communion has been shared and the benediction pronounced, he meets the one he had come to consider an adversary in the aisle. They exchange a handshake and a look, a look that says, "Rejection transformed."

Rejection transformed. It is God's gracious, marvelous gift to us.

SUGGESTIONS FOR WORSHIP

Call to Worship

LEADER: We ponder your steadfast love, O God, in the midst of your Temple.

PEOPLE: **Your name, O God, like your praise, reaches to the ends of the earth.**

Prayer of Confession

Wise God, we shrink from offering the totality of our lives to you. Vulnerability to your word and your ways makes us fearful, and so we hold back parts of ourselves from your life and love. Forgive us, and help us open all aspects of our lives to you. Shape us into a people through whom you can do a mighty work.

Assurance of Pardon

Paul says that "When we were dead through our trespasses, [God] made us alive together with Christ" (Eph. 2:5*a*). Let us claim with assurance, then, our forgiveness and new life in Christ.

Benediction

Brothers and sisters, put things in order. Agree with one another. Live in peace, and the God of love and peace be with you.

Ordinary Time 17 or Proper 12

Elizabeth McGregor Simmons

---

2 Samuel 11:1-15: David commits adultery with Bathsheba and sends her husband Uriah to the front lines to be killed.

Psalm 14: To deny the reality of God is ultimate foolishness.

Ephesians 3:14-21: In exultant, praise-filled tones, the writer prays for those who read the letter.

John 6:1-21: Jesus presides over the feeding of the multitude of five thousand. During the evening, he comes to the disciples on the sea.

REFLECTIONS

Riding in the front seat of a rental van crammed with fourteen teenagers as we made our twenty-hour trek home from a denominational youth conference, I was shamelessly eavesdropping on their conversation when it occurred to me that they were spending more time than they probably realized discussing what they didn't have, how much they wanted it, and how they planned to get it. The teens talked about clothes, CDs, and cars. We adults shift the subject matter to the stock market, real estate, and, well, cars; but we, too, are prone to complain about scarcity, even in the midst of great material abundance.

It is of some comfort to realize that we are not the first to exhibit this symptom of spiritual impoverishment. "If only we had died by the hand of the Lord in the land of Egypt . . . ; for you have brought us out into this wilderness to kill this whole assembly with hunger," the Israelites had carped to Moses (Exodus 16:3). Something in Philip's response to Jesus when confronted with a large crowd of hungry people must have reminded the Gospel writer of the Israelites' complaint, for there are traces of the Old Testament story of Yahweh's provision of manna shimmering throughout John 6. Images such as the mountain, Passover, bread from heaven, and the murmuring of the people provide important clues for assimilating the Gospel story into our lives.

A SERMON BRIEF

"Six months' wages would not buy enough bread for each person here to get even one teeny-weeny bite!" Philip whines to Jesus. Philip is complaining about scarcity, and in his whining and carping and complaining, I have to admit that I hear echoes of my own.

One would think that I, as a child growing up in a secure middle-class home, would not have had cause to complain about scarcity. I, however, have a passion, and that passion is Krispy Kreme doughnuts. If you have ever lived or traveled in the South and tasted a Krispy Kreme doughnut, then you know what I'm talking about. A Krispy Kreme doughnut served dripping with its warm sugary glaze, melting the split-second it hits your tongue, deserves its own exhibit in the Smithsonian, which it just happens to have earned recently.

Whenever my father would go to town for a meeting, he would always make one last stop on his way home—at the Krispy Kreme doughnut shop to pick up one dozen doughnuts. The only problem was that there were seven of us. That's how we learned fractions at our house, dividing twelve doughnuts by seven people: a sliver less than one and three-quarters per person.

But sometimes someone would sneak stealthily into the kitchen in the dark of night, and when we trooped into the kitchen for breakfast the next morning and opened the green and white lid of the doughnut box, we uncovered the dastardly deed: Someone had eaten a whole doughnut rather than carefully calculating his or her three-quarters-doughnut allotment. Then the whining and carping and complaining would start bouncing off the walls: "Who did this? It's not fair. There's not going to be enough for me."

Philip complained about scarcity. So did the McGregor kids. And so do many of us, particularly us Americans, I think. Will there be enough in my bank account at the end of the month to pay the bills? Will there be enough to send my children to college? Will there be enough to see me through retirement? Will there be enough love in this relationship? Will there be enough time today, this week, in my whole life to get everything done? We look at the world and at life itself with the same assumption that underlies Philip's words: No, there isn't enough. There isn't enough money, enough time, enough love to meet all the needs that clamor around us.

What, then, does the gospel say to those who live life with the assumption that there is simply not enough to go around? What does it say to the primal fear that haunts many of us more than we sometimes even know, the fear that there may not be enough for everybody, there may not be enough for those whom I love, and most especially, there may not be enough for me? In answer to these questions, Jesus' feeding of five thousand people offers us a deep and central truth.

The occasion of the feeding of the five thousand is an important event. The account of its occurrence is recorded in all four Gospels. There is, however, a distinctive difference in John's telling of the story. While the synoptic Gospels—Matthew, Mark, and Luke—recount the way in which Jesus was moved by compassion to feed the hungry, John does not reflect this motive at all. Rather, in John's version, Jesus seems most intent upon teaching the disciples something that they will need to understand if they are to carry on his ministry when he is no longer with them physically.

This "something," this central truth that he wishes to impart to them, is the understanding that life, when lived in the gracious power of God, is a place of abundance, not scarcity. This flashing light on the highway of faith is a theme to which Jesus returns often in the Gospel of John. "I came that they might have life, and have it abundantly" (John 10:10), he says; and he demonstrates it in many different ways, over and over again.

This is the central truth that Jesus reveals when he transforms a snack into a banquet on the grassy knoll on the side of the mountain. Performing this "sign," as it is called, is his way of grabbing the disciples and us by the lapels, looking us straight in the eye, and saying, "Don't miss this. This is something you need to know. Look around you. Open your eyes and look, really look at how the holy presence of God has the power to transform life."

Nearly everything in our culture certainly, perhaps even in our human nature, bucks and strains against our recognizing that life is abundant. A man who leads travel tours to Europe was talking about his sense of frustration on a recent tour. "When we arrived in London," he said, "everybody immediately began reading brochures about Paris. When we got to Paris, they all unpacked their books on

Rome, and when we got to Rome, they all took out their airline tickets to study their itinerary back to Indianapolis. Everywhere they were, they were not there" (George Ross, quoted in Leonard Sweet, *Strong in the Broken Places: A Theological Reverie on the Ministry of George Everett Ross* [Akron, Ohio: University of Akron Press, 1995], 209).

Those travelers, I fear, were living out of a sense of life's scarcity. Caught up in some ephemeral sense of not having enough, they simply could not allow themselves to be where they were, to be open to graciousness and the abundance of the moment.

There is, however, another way of living, a way Jesus clearly demonstrates as he feeds the five thousand. The feeding of the five thousand didn't happen only once. It didn't happen only in the first century, only on a mountain in Galilee. By the grace of God, it is happening all around us and within us.

It is happening when a child takes her dollar allowance and drops it into an offering envelope for world hunger instead of spending it on a snack at the pool. It is happening when a teenager spends an afternoon at a nursing home, visiting a neighbor who is recuperating from a stroke, instead of making a trek to the mall. It is happening when a person ignores a deadline and leaves work to respond to a friend's phone call pleading that she "just needs to talk to someone." It is happening when someone skips dinner one night a week to go to a prison to listen and to pray with the inmates incarcerated there. It is happening when hungry people are fed, when the walls of race and national identity and economic class that serve to separate people come tumbling down, when healing of mind, body, or spirit occurs. This is life, abundant life, and if we are willing to open our eyes and hearts to the wonder and wisdom and power and presence of our God who is revealed to us in Jesus Christ, we will come to understand. We have more than enough.

SUGGESTIONS FOR WORSHIP

Call to Worship (adapted from John 6:32-35)

LEADER: Jesus said, "Very truly, I tell you, it was not Moses who gave you the bread from heaven, but it is my Father who gives you the true bread from heaven. For the bread of God is that which comes down from heaven, and gives life to the world."

PEOPLE: **Lord, give us this bread always.**

LEADER: Jesus then said, "I am the bread of life. Whoever comes to me will never be hungry, and whoever believes in me will never be thirsty."

Prayer of Confession

Gracious God, we confess that we are sometimes haunted by a sense of scarcity. We fear that we won't have enough, materially and spiritually. Forgive us, and grant us an understanding of how abundant your love truly is.

Assurance of Pardon
(adapted from Ezekiel 36:26, 28-29)

LEADER: "A new heart I will give you, and a new spirit I will put within you; and I will remove from your body the heart of stone and give you a heart of flesh. Then you shall live in the land that I gave to your ancestors; and you shall be my people, and I will be your God. I will save you from all your uncleannesses, and I will summon the grain and make it abundant and lay no famine upon you."

PEOPLE: **In the name of Jesus Christ, the bread of heaven, we accept the gift of abundant life.**

Benediction (adapted from Ephesians 3:17-19)

May "Christ dwell in your hearts through faith, as you are being rooted and grounded in love." May you "know the love of Christ that surpasses knowledge, so that you may be filled with all the fullness of God."

Ordinary Time 26 or Proper 21

Felicia Y. Thomas

Esther 7:1-6, 9-10; 9:20-22: The Jews are delivered from Haman's wicked plot as a result of Esther's bravery. The feast of Purim is established.

Psalm 124: A song of thanksgiving for divine intervention and Israel's deliverance from its enemies.

James 5:13-20: A teaching about the efficacy of prayer and confession in restoring the community of faith.

Mark 9:38-50: "Whoever is not against us is for us."

REFLECTIONS

It is not always easy to know who is for us or who is against us. And when we manage to figure out just who is who and what is what, there is the question of what, if anything, we should or can do about it. The Old Testament readings for this Sunday instruct us to rely on God's power and aid to withstand enemy attack. The New Testament readings urge us to be allies of one another in faith, lest we become stumbling blocks and fail to enter the realm of God.

A SERMON BRIEF

This Sunday's Gospel lesson begins with John reporting an incident to Jesus in which the disciples tried to stop an outsider from casting out demons in the name of Jesus. A number of plausible motives for John's course of action come to mind:

The desire for approval and affirmation. Perhaps John wanted Jesus to know that he and his fellow disciples were on top of things; they were protecting Jesus' interests from interlopers and potential frauds.

Self-interest. John may have been protecting his own hide. He had probably decided that Jesus would not be pleased by this development, and he did not want to be chastised for failing to act.

Insecurity. John may have felt threatened by the success of others, especially outsiders.

Jealousy. It probably is not a coincidence that John and the other disciples were trying to forbid the man from doing what they had failed to do: namely, cast out demons (see Mark 9:18). The outsider's ability to accomplish what they could not might call their power and authority into question.

In light of such possibilities, Jesus' response to John is all the more intriguing:

Do not stop him. Jesus lets John and the other disciples know that their handling of this situation is off-base.

Nobody can use my name to do a miracle one minute and slander me in the next. Jesus says this to draw a contrast between the outsider and the scribes, who had accused Jesus of being demon possessed.

Whoever is not against us is for us. Jesus uses this proverb to challenge John and the other disciples not to be a closed society, but to cultivate a spirit of tolerance and acceptance.

In this encounter, John and the other disciples fail to take Jesus' mission and purpose into account. Jesus was not interested in opening a chapel or starting a club. Jesus was not interested in forbidding or excluding. Jesus came to bring good news to the poor and relief to the oppressed. Jesus came to encourage the hopeless and befriend the friendless. Jesus came to lift bowed heads and to break the grip of sin and disease. Jesus came to proclaim the wideness of God's love.

Jesus came not to build walls but to break down barriers. Jesus came to establish a kingdom in which every member would be affirmed and cared for. The disciples missed this entirely in their efforts to keep an outsider from living out his faith in the power of God in Christ. The disciples lost sight of the one who was demon-possessed, and who needed deliverance and who did not care whether it came from an authorized source, as long as it came. The disciples failed to realize that no one who cast out demons in the name of Jesus posed a threat to their livelihood and well-being.

This text challenges us to examine our responses to the good efforts of those who either by choice or necessity do not fall within the sphere of our influence. As Christians we are called to be open and receptive to *good news* wherever we find it. We are charged with supporting and affirming the gospel, whether or not we authorized, organized, or sponsored the vehicle by which it is spread.

It is sad that so many of our churches have become gated communities in which there is little or no openness to new ideas, new methods, or new people. Many churches have adopted a fortress mentality. But a fortress does not invite visitors, neither is it a good platform for outreach. Fortress outreach is half-hearted at best. More often it is nonexistent. Institutions with fortress mentalities soon lose their vitality and viability. Eventually they crumble from within.

Obviously, the disciples had forgotten that before Jesus extended the invitation to them, they had been outsiders. They had no standing within the community. In fact, some of them were despised. They had no power. Yet Jesus recognized their need and their potential. He called them and accepted them. He gave them a sense of meaning and purpose. He enabled them to have a significant part in the building of his kingdom.

Many of us have had a similar experience of Christ's presence in our lives. And that experience must not be used as the basis for hindering others or for shutting them out. If we act in an exclusionary way, we miss the point and run the risk of forfeiting the kingdom that we want so much to establish.

It takes more faith and courage to embrace outsiders and welcome strangers than it takes to insulate ourselves with false piety. It takes more love to tolerate diversity than it does to insist on homogeneity. It takes tremendous hope to greet those outside our circle with confidence and grace, rather than insecurity and fear.

Praise be to God for the faith, courage, hope, and love that we have in Christ. Let us not get sidetracked with concerns about who is out and who is in, but let us be expansive in our witness, to the end that all might know Christ's power to save.

SUGGESTIONS FOR WORSHIP

Call to Worship

We acknowledge your presence in our midst, blessed Lord. Touch us with your love and grace as we gather together to praise and worship you.

Prayer of Confession

Merciful teacher, forgive us for our tendencies toward short-sightedness and narrow-mindedness. We want to be bigger than we are—more tolerant, more supportive, and more accepting of one another. But we need your help. Strengthen us where we are weak. Open us where we are closed. Fill us where we are empty. Challenge us where we are complacent. Urge us where we are stagnant. Inspire us with visions of your kingdom. In your name. Amen.

Assurance of Pardon

God's mercy is wide and deep. Within it we find forgiveness and peace. Thanks be to God. Amen.

Benediction

Blessed be God. Our help is in God, our creator. Our hope is in Christ, our redeemer. Our joy is in the Spirit, our sustainer. Send us forth with open minds and open hearts. Empower us to embrace and accept all your children. To your glory and in your name. Amen.

Contributors

Catherine Erskine Boileau, Pastor of Mt. Nebo and Mt. Olivet United Methodist Churches in Delta, Pennsylvania. An ordained elder in the United Methodist Church, Cathy enjoys the challenge of caring for two churches, two preschoolers, one husband, and a golden retriever named Pickle. Cathy's first invitation to preach came fourteen years ago at a Christmas Eve service when "I didn't know enough to be nervous. It was at that moment, when I stepped into that pulpit, that I knew why God had created me—to preach."

Linda McKinnish Bridges, Professor of New Testament and Greek at the Baptist Theological Seminary in Richmond, Virginia. Linda, whose scholarly interests include Johannine literature and the role of women in Celtic Christian traditions, was one of the founding members of the Baptist Theological Seminary in Virginia and of the Center for Women in Christian Leadership in Richmond. A dynamic teacher and preacher, she is mother to Kyle, "a wonderful twelve-year-old soccer player and Star Wars fan," and wife to Tilden, "Baptist minister and fantastic father." She enjoys music, poetry, good novels, the North Carolina mountains, good food (that her friends prepare), and good preaching.

Valerie Brown-Troutt, Associate Pastor and Christian Education Director at the City of Refuge Community Church (United Church of Christ), Deputy Executive Director of the Ark of Refuge, and CEO of Refuge Ministries, Inc., in San Francisco, California. Valerie speaks of herself as a "survivor" who has a passion for working with marginalized groups and reinforcing survivor principles of self-care and self-esteem. A life partner and wife for twenty-seven years, she is the mother of five children.

Rhonda VanDyke Colby, Pastor of Good Shepherd United Methodist Church in Richmond, Virginia. During Rhonda's six years as pastor, Good Shepherd Church has grown from a small membership to a multiple staff church. Rhonda also served as founding director of Harvest of Hope, a hunger education and gleaning program, and as founder of the Elizabeth Project, a mentoring program for pregnant teens. With her husband Don (also a UMC clergyperson) Rhonda reports that she is enjoying the "thrill ride" of parenting Anna (sixteen), Drew (thirteen), and Austin (ten).

Joan Delaplane, O.P., Professor of Homiletics (since 1977) at Aquinas Institute of Theology, St. Louis, Missouri. Joan is a Dominican Sister of Adrian, Michigan, and was the first Roman Catholic and the first woman to serve as President of the Academy of Homiletics. The very first volume of *The Abingdon Women's Preaching Annual* (Series 1, Year B) was dedicated to Joan as one of the "mothers of homiletics." Joan, who loves to dance, says of the Academy of Homiletics, "That's where the dancing began!"

Joan Dennehy, Pastor of Findlay Street Christian Church (Disciples of Christ) in Seattle, Washington, the first "open and affirming" congregation of her denomination. Ordained eleven years ago, Joan was previously a stained-glass artist. She is also the mother of five grown children. Joan has a passion for story and devotes her work to re-imaging cultural and spiritual myths, saying, "It is time for humanity to make a significant leap in evolution if we are sustain our planet and one another."

Anna Carter Florence, Assistant Professor of Preaching at Columbia Theological Seminary in Decatur, Georgia. An ordained Presbyterian minister and native New Englander, Anna previously served as a pastor in Minnesota and has been the featured preacher in numerous settings, including "The Protestant Hour" radio program. When she isn't teaching or working on her doctoral dissertation, Anna can be found at the playground with her two spirited young sons, or composting the garden with her pastor husband.

Yvette Flunder, Senior Pastor, City of Refuge Community Church, United Church of Christ in San Francisco, California. Yvette's ministry passion is to develop a viable Christian community among those who are on the margins of church and society. To that end she has established a variety of outreach ministries in San Francisco, where she also serves on the city's Parks and Recreation Commission. Yvette says she owes her commitment to ministry among the marginalized and her hand-clapping Pentecostal worship style to the influence of her "church-building" parents and grandparents.

Eunjoo Mary Kim, Assistant Professor of Homiletics, Iliff School of Theology in Denver, Colorado. An ordained Presbyterian minister, Eunjoo has served as pastor and copastor in several Korean American congregations in New Jersey. She was one of the first Asians in the world to hold a Ph.D. degree in the field of homiletics, and the first Asian in this country to hold a full-time tenured position as a professor of homiletics. In her recent book, *A Homiletic from the Asian-American Perspective*, Eunjoo makes cross-cultural connections related to the formation and nurture of Christian spirituality through preaching.

Alyce M. McKenzie, Assistant Professor of Preaching at Perkins School of Theology in Dallas, Texas. Alyce, an ordained elder in the United Methodist Church since 1982, served as Associate Pastor of Aldersgate United Methodist Church in York, Pennsylvania, before pursuing her Ph.D. in homiletics. In recent years she has led a number of continuing education events for pastors while also teaching preaching on an adjunct basis at Princeton Theological Seminary and serving as interim pastor for several churches in the Eastern Pennsylvania Conference. A wife and mother of three, Alyce enjoys taking long walks, reading whodunits, and cheering on her son's soccer team.

Mary Alice Mulligan, Pastor of Central Christian Church (Disciples of Christ) in Indianapolis, Indiana. Mary Alice is not only a pastor, but also a Ph.D. candidate in homiletics and ethics at Vanderbilt University. She says her dissertation will be completed not only through her hard work, but

170

through the grace of God, the patience of her son, the support of her parents, and the persistent encouragement of her beloved. For each she is eternally grateful.

Adele Stiles Resmer, Assistant Professor of Homiletics at the Lutheran Theological Seminary in Philadelphia, Pennsylvania. An ordained minister in the Evangelical Lutheran Church in America, Adele is the founder of the ELCA's Steering Committee on AIDS and cofounder of the Lutheran AIDS Network. She brings to her teaching and preaching a rich background in the study of Christian ethics.

Margaret K. Schwarzer, Episcopal Chaplain at Boston University. Margaret was ordained five years ago at Trinity Church in Princeton, New Jersey, where she served as the Assistant Minister until her move to Boston. She says that she learned to relish the challenge of preaching because of her parents, who taught her about the power in the art of storytelling, and the power at the heart of love.

Elizabeth McGregor Simmons, Pastor of University Presbyterian Church in San Antonio, Texas. Since her ordination in 1979, Lib has served congregations in Jacksonville, Florida, and St. Louis, Missouri, before moving to her present position in San Antonio. She comments, "The members of these churches have been my teachers through their patience and honesty. They, along with my parents, my three brothers and my one sister, my husband Gary, and my son, Mac, have made me a minister."

Felicia Y. Thomas, Pastor of First Baptist Church in Princeton, New Jersey. Felicia is the first woman to serve as pastor of this historic African American congregation. *Ebony* magazine recently named her one of the outstanding African American preachers in the United States. In life and ministry Felicia says she is nurtured by the love and support of her husband, mother, and two young sons. She enjoys walking, reading, and visiting with friends whenever she has the opportunity.

Leonora Tubbs Tisdale, Associate Professor of Preaching and Worship, Princeton Theological Seminary, Princeton, New Jersey. Nora served as a pastor of four congregations in Virginia and as a volunteer missionary (teaching in a seminary in Seoul, Korea) before going into full-time seminary teaching in 1988. She is the author of *Preaching as Local Theology and Folk Art* (Fortress Press, 1997), a book voted one of the top ten books of the year for parish pastors by the Academy of Parish Clergy. Nora has a special passion for helping women develop their gifts as preachers, and has taught a number of courses related to women and preaching. Her pastor husband, Al, and two teenage children, Leonora and William, are sources of great joy in her life.

Dawn Ottoni Wilhelm, Assistant Professor of Ministry Studies at Bethany Theological Seminary in Richmond, Indiana. Since the time of her baptism at age nineteen, Dawn has found her home in the Church of the Brethren. She has previously served as a hospital chaplain, as adjunct seminary faculty, and as a pastor in several congregations—most recently serving as Senior Pastor of the Stone Church of the Brethren in Huntingdon, Pennsylvania. Currently on leave from her teaching duties, Dawn is pursuing a Ph.D. degree in preaching at Princeton Theological Seminary while also caring for her three young children. She enjoys classical music and hymnody, as well as the company of her husband.

Gláucia Vasconcelos Wilkey, Associate for Worship for the Presbyterian Church (USA), Louisville, Kentucky. Gláucia, an ordained minister and native of Brazil, holds graduate degrees in theology, education, and music. Before coming to her current position in 1995, she served as a seminary professor in Brazil (teaching church music and education), as a missionary to Portugese-speaking people in Canada, and as an Associate Pastor in two U.S. congregations. Gláucia, who has a passion for enhancing the worship and music life of local congregations, has led many workshops and conferences in Brazil, Canada, and the United States. She is married to Dr. Jay Wilkey, a voice professor and church musician.

Scripture Index

Subject Index